USING Microsoft® Works

Nelda Shelton
South Campus
Tarrant County Junior College District

Sharon Burton
Brookhaven College
Dallas County Community College District

HOUGHTON MIFFLIN COMPANY   BOSTON

Dallas   Geneva, Illinois   Palo Alto   Princeton, New Jersey

Printing History
First Printing, January 1988
Second printing, August 1988
Third printing, April 1989

ISBN: 0-395-47794-8

Printed in the U.S.A.

IJ-SM-965432

▬▬▬Contents

Publisher's Foreword

This book is in the Houghton Mifflin Software Solutions Series. The series is explicitly designed to offer solutions to the problems encountered by educators who wish to include instruction on popular commercial application software programs as a component of courses they teach.

The purpose of this series is to provide high quality, inexpensive—in fact, remarkably inexpensive—tutorial manuals keyed to the leading software packages available.

Instructionally Innovative

Each manual in the Software Solutions Series focuses on those features of a particular program that will actually be used by most individuals. The manuals do not purport to teach everything there is to know about the product; to do that, the manual would have to be needlessly complex and would impose unrealistic time constraints on both students and instructors. The manuals will enable students to attain comfortable proficiency in the use of software products.

Flexible

The Software Solutions Series permits instructors to choose the manuals that best suit their needs. This offers an important advantage over those manuals that combine coverage of several programs in a single publication and thus limit flexibility.

Cost

Students enrolled in a computer literacy or business data processing course often require lab-based instruction on the use of three or more application programs, usually a word processing program, a database manager, and a spreadsheet program. This common course configuration can impose a financial burden on students if they must purchase three expensive manuals in addition to the primary course text. We believe the Software Solutions Series goes a long way toward solving this problem by providing an effective and inexpensive method for learning about software.

High Quality

All manuals in the Software Solutions Series are authored by writers who have teaching experience in the classroom and in training programs in business and industry. Each manual in the series has been reviewed for accuracy and pedagogical effectiveness.

Software Program Disks

The Software Solutions Series currently consists of eleven manuals and software for the following products: Microsoft Works, WordPerfect 4.2, WordStar, dBASE III Plus, SuperCalc 4, Lotus 1-2-3, WordPerfect 5.0, Microsoft Word, MS-DOS, dBase IV, and PageMaker.

Master disks containing educational versions of Microsoft Works, WordPerfect, WordStar, dBASE III Plus, and SuperCalc 4 are available from Houghton Mifflin without charge to adopters of the manuals. These disks may be duplicated for individual student use by instructors in accordance with applicable license agreements.

For Lotus 1-2-3, WordPerfect 5.0, Microsoft Word, MS-DOS, dBase IV, and PageMaker, data disks rather than educational versions of the program disks are available from Houghton Mifflin without charge to adopters.

All manuals in the Software Solutions Series and their accompanying disks are for use with IBM equipment except for PageMaker, which is only for the Macintosh.

We wish to thank Microsoft Corporation, WordPerfect Corporation, MicroPro International, Computer Associates, and Ashton-Tate for their cooperation in helping to make this series available.

Preface

USING MICROSOFT WORKS introduces the student to one of the newest and most powerful integrated application programs available today. The package makes it easy for students to learn the basics of Microsoft Works in a very short period of time. It does so by building on the natural learning process so that students avoid frustration and confusion. This sharp focus allows students to develop an understanding of how Microsoft Works functions and to issue commands confidently to achieve useful results—all within a reasonable time.

Pedagogical features that ensure mastery of the basics in a short period of time are an integral part of each chapter.

■ An introduction explains features covered in the chapter.

■ New terminology is presented at the beginning of each chapter.

■ Step-by-step instructions are followed by an illustrated example and practice exercises that allow students to use each feature in a hands-on environment.

■ Every exercise step number is enclosed in a box, making it easy for students to identify what they are to read and what they are to do.

■ Frequent illustrations make it easy for students to check their work as they go along, building their confidence and understanding and providing positive reinforcement.

■ Tips give students important shortcuts and reminders as well as directions and explanations.

■ Each chapter ends with a summary of the concepts and commands presented in the chapter; this encourages review and mastery of the basics.

■ Four appendixes provide a summary of commands, information on using a hard disk, formatting commands, and a menu summary.

The manual's step-by-step instructions complement the classroom-tested Read and Do approach to teaching. After reading a simple explanation of a new concept and studying an example, students complete an exercise on the computer. This logical presentation means that students focus on one feature at a time, are guided through an exercise in which they practice using the feature under discussion, and complete the exercise on their own—gaining confidence as they complete the performance of each new feature. Clear hands-on instructions walk students through each new element of the program, and illustrations showing correct screens or printed output allow them to check their work as they go along.

Because this manual is designed to give first-time users basic competence in using the program, advanced Microsoft Works features are not covered. Seven text chapters teach the basics for using the word processing, spreadsheet, database, and communication components of this powerful program.

A disk containing the educational version of Microsoft Works, Release 1.0, which can be copied, is supplied to instructors who adopt this manual. The educational version of the software has been limited in the following ways:

1. No documentation, printer or plotter drivers other than TTY and Epson FX are supplied. Choose the Epson FX printer if you have an Epson FX or a printer than emulates one. Otherwise, choose TTY, which will emulate most other printers. Epson FX is the default.

2. Certain chart fonts, the spelling checker, help disk, computer-based tutorials, and macros are not included. Help Index and Tutorial Index will appear on the window menu in each tool but are not included with the Educational Version of the software.

3. The maximum file size for the word processor is 25K, between five pages (with dense formatting) and 10 pages (with sparse formatting) of text. Neither the spreadsheet nor the database can exceed 32 columns by 256 rows with a maximum column width of 79 characters. Although the educational version of Microsoft Works will not save or open files that exceed these size limitations, the program does read and write files compatible with the full retail version.

4. No other commands have been removed. Except as noted in 1 and 2 above, the educational version is as functional as the full retail version.

Students may store their work directly on the program disks, or they may format data disks of their own. If they choose to save files on the program disk, it will be necessary to delete files as the disk fills. To delete a file, exit to DOS (ALT, F, D, press ENTER). When the A:> appears, type: erase (name of file), then press Enter for each file to be deleted. To return to Works, type: exit. If students choose to store their work on separate data disks, they will have to switch disks in the A drive if they have only a single drive or put the data disk in drive B and precede all document names with B: if they have a dual-floppy system. Students may also copy their program disks to a hard drive. Instructions for using this software on a hard-disk system are found in Appendix B. This text assumes students will save all files onto a data disk of their own using a two-disk drive system.

Your program disk contains five screendriver files: EGA.GSD, HER-CULES.GSD, MCGA.GSD, and TANDY.GSD. Depending on the type of graphics card you have installed, you will need to rename one of these files so that you may later display charts on your screen. Before copying and/or loading the Using Microsoft Works disk, select and rename the appropriate screendriver file to SCREEN. GSD. For example, if you are using a CGA interface you will need to do the following:

1. Load DOS.

2. Remove the DOS disk and insert the Microsoft Works disk.

3. Type RENAME CGA. GSD SCREEN. GSD

To use this package, you must have the following:

■ A copy of the Microsoft Works Educational Version master disk supplied to instructors adopting this manual

■ An IBM-PC or compatible computer or an IBM Personal System/2 series computer that uses double-sided floppy disks

■ At least 384K RAM (Random Access Memory)

■ MS or PC DOS 2.0 or higher

■ Two 320K or one 720K disk drive; a hard (fixed) disk system may be used

■ CGA, EGA, MCGA, VGA, or Hercules graphics adapter for charting

■ A standard monitor or an IBM Enhanced Color Display monitor

■ A color or black and white graphics printer

- A Hayes-compatible modem and/or Microsoft Mouse optional
- Formatted 5.25" or 3.5" disks for backing up the program disk and storing data

Acknowledgments

In writing textbook materials, authors need the help of a number of individuals.

We would like to thank Kaye Davis, Brookhaven College, for her tips and attention to detail. Her many hours spent working through the manuscript are greatly appreciated.

A word of appreciation goes to Mary Jane Tobaben, Brookhaven College, for reading the manuscript and testing the practice exercises.

Thank you goes to Vickie Crider and Lori Leyendecker, students at Tarrant County Junior College—South Campus, for checking the materials.

End-user Agreement

Houghton Mifflin Company End-User and Limited Reproduction Rights License Agreement for Teachers and Students

HOUGHTON MIFFLIN COMPANY SOFTWARE LICENSE

READ THIS FIRST. Your use of the Microsoft software (the "SOFTWARE") is governed by the legal agreement below. If you are a teacher and you receive a diskette with your copy of this book, your use of the SOFTWARE is governed by both sections I and II. If you are a student and you are receiving a copy of the teacher's diskette, your use of the SOFTWARE is governed by only section II.

I. HOUGHTON MIFFLIN COMPANY LIMITED REPRODUCTION RIGHTS LICENSE AGREEMENT FOR TEACHERS

BY OPENING THE SEALED DISK PACKAGE, YOU ARE AGREEING TO BE BOUND BY THE TERMS AND CONDITIONS IN BOTH SECTIONS I AND II OF THIS AGREEMENT. IF YOU DO NOT AGREE TO SUCH TERMS AND CONDITIONS, PROMPTLY RETURN THE UNOPENED DISK PACKAGE TOGETHER WITH THE BOOK TO THE PLACE WHERE YOU OBTAINED THEM FOR A REFUND.

1. If you are a teacher and you are using this Book for educational purposes, you may make limited copies of the SOFTWARE on the following conditions only:

(a) You must first notify each student receiving such copy that his or her use of the SOFTWARE is governed by the end-user license agreement as contained in section II below.

(b) You must make only one copy of the SOFTWARE copy per copy of the Book purchased or owned by the student. STUDENTS ARE *NOT* AUTHORIZED BY THIS AGREEMENT OR OTHERWISE TO MAKE COPIES OF THE SOFT-

WARE, EXCEPT AS PROVIDED IN THE END-USER LICENSE AGREE-
MENT BELOW.

(c) If you make any additional copies of the SOFTWARE, you are violating the terms of this Agreement that you have signed, and you will risk legal penalties against you.

II. HOUGHTON MIFFLIN COMPANY END-USER LICENSE AGREEMENT

Students:

BY ACCEPTING THE COPIED SOFTWARE FROM YOUR TEACHER, YOU ARE AGREEING TO BE BOUND BY THE TERMS AND CONDITIONS BELOW IN THIS SECTION II. IF YOU DO NOT AGREE WITH SUCH TERMS AND CONDITIONS, YOU SHOULD RETURN THE SOFTWARE TO YOUR TEACHER TOGETHER WITH THE BOOK.

1. *GRANT OF LICENSE.* Houghton Mifflin Company grants to you the right to use one copy of the enclosed SOFTWARE on a single terminal connected to a single computer (i.e. with a single CPU). You must not network the SOFTWARE or otherwise use it on more than one computer or computer terminal at the same time.

2. *COPYRIGHT.* The SOFTWARE is owned by Microsoft or its suppliers and is protected by United States copyright laws and international treaty provisions. Therefore, you must treat the SOFTWARE like any other copyrighted material (e.g. a book or musical recording) except that you may either (a) make one copy of the SOFTWARE solely for backup or archival purposes, or (b) transfer the SOFTWARE to a single hard disk provided you keep the original solely for backup or archival purposes. You may not copy the written materials.

3. *OTHER RESTRICTIONS.* You may not rent or lease the SOFTWARE, but you may transfer the SOFTWARE and written materials on a permanent basis provided you retain no copies and the recipient agrees to the terms of this Agreement. You may not reverse engineer, decompile or disassemble the SOFTWARE.

4. *DUAL MEDIA SOFTWARE.* If the SOFTWARE package contains both 3 1/2" and 5 1/4" disks, then you may use only the disks appropriate for your single-user computer. You may not use the other disks on another computer or loan, rent, lease, or transfer them to another user except as part of the permanent transfer (as provided above) of all SOFTWARE and written materials.

DISCLAIMER OF WARRANTY AND LIMITED WARRANTY

THE SOFTWARE AND ACCOMPANYING WRITTEN MATERIALS (INCLUDING INSTRUCTIONS FOR USE) ARE PROVIDED "AS IS" WITHOUT WARRANTY OF ANY KIND. FURTHER, HOUGHTON MIFFLIN COMPANY DOES NOT WARRANT, GUARANTEE, OR MAKE ANY REPRESENTATIONS REGARDING THE USE, OR THE RESULTS OF THE USE, OF THE SOFTWARE OR WRITTEN MATERIALS IN TERMS OF CORRECTNESS, ACCURACY, RELIA-

BILITY, CURRENTNESS, OR OTHERWISE. THE ENTIRE RISK AS TO THE RE-
SULTS AND PERFORMANCE OF THE SOFTWARE IS ASSUMED BY YOU. IF
THE SOFTWARE OR WRITTEN MATERIALS ARE DEFECTIVE YOU, AND NOT
HOUGHTON MIFFLIN COMPANY OR ITS DEALERS, DISTRIBUTORS,
AGENTS, OR EMPLOYEES, ASSUME THE ENTIRE COST OF ALL NECESSARY
SERVICING, REPAIR OR CORRECTION.

Houghton Mifflin Company warrants to the original LICENSEE that (a) the
disk(s) on which the SOFTWARE is recorded is free from defects in materials and
workmanship under normal use and service for a period of ninety (90) days from
the date of delivery as evidenced by a copy of the receipt. Further, Houghton
Mifflin Company hereby limits the duration of any implied warranty(ies) on the
disk to the respective periods stated above. Some states do not allow limitations
on duration of an implied warranty, so the above limitation may not apply to you.

Houghton Mifflin Company's entire liability and your exclusive remedy as to
the disk(s) shall be at Houghton Mifflin's option, either (a) return of the purchase
price or (b) replacement of the disk that does not meet Houghton Mifflin Company's Limited Warranty and which is returned to Houghton Mifflin Company with
a copy of the receipt. If failure of the disk has resulted from accident, abuse, or
misapplication, Houghton Mifflin Company shall have no responsibility to replace the disk or refund the purchase price. Any replacement disk will be war-
ranted for the remainder of the original warranty period of thirty (30) days,
whichever is longer.

NO OTHER WARRANTIES. HOUGHTON MIFFLIN COMPANY DISCLAIMS
ALL OTHER WARRANTIES, EITHER EXPRESS OR IMPLIED, INCLUDING BUT
NOT LIMITED TO IMPLIED WARRANTIES OF MERCHANTABILITY AND FIT-
NESS FOR A PARTICULAR PURPOSE, WITH RESPECT TO THE SOFTWARE,
THE ACCOMPANYING HARDWARE. THIS LIMITED WARRANTY GIVES
YOU SPECIFIC LEGAL RIGHTS. YOU MAY HAVE OTHERS, WHICH VARY
FROM STATE TO STATE.

NO LIABILITY FOR CONSEQUENTIAL DAMAGES. IN NO EVENT SHALL
HOUGHTON MIFFLIN COMPANY OR ITS SUPPLIERS BE LIABLE FOR ANY
DAMAGES WHATSOEVER (INCLUDING WITHOUT LIMITATION DAMAGES
FOR LOSS OF BUSINESS PROFITS, BUSINESS INTERRUPTION, LOSS OF
BUSINESS INFORMATION, OR OTHER PECUNIARY LOSS) ARISING OUT OF
THE USE OR INABILITY TO USE THIS MICROSOFT PRODUCT EVEN IF
HOUGHTON MIFFLIN COMPANY HAS BEEN ADVISED OF THE POSSIBLILI-
TY OF SUCH DAMAGES. BECAUSE SOME STATES DO NOT ALLOW THE EX-
CLUSION OR LIMITATION OF LIABILITY FOR CONSEQUENTIAL OR INCI-
DENTAL DAMAGES, THE ABOVE LIMITATION MAY NOT APPLY TO YOU.

1

Learning About Your
IBM PC

Welcome to the IBM PC and *Microsoft Works!* So that you will be more efficient in using *Works*, take a few minutes to become acquainted with the IBM Personal Computer. For specific instructions on its use, refer to the *IBM PC Guide to Operations*, to DOS manuals, or to any other training materials you have.

Do not be intimidated by the computer. It is simply a sophisticated tool that saves time and improves your efficiency and productivity in handling information. Before you begin, however, you should know that learning to use *Works* on your IBM PC involves paying attention to details, as well as practicing.

The presentation in this manual follows the same basic information (with a few exceptions) used in the *Microsoft Works Reference* manual.

This chapter acquaints you with the basic terminology and components of your computer system.

Terminology

Knowing some basic terms will help you understand the IBM PC and its operation. Here are some of these terms.

Hardware means the physical parts of the computer.

Software means the programs that run on the computer. *Programs* are sets of instructions. The program tells the computer what to do, when to do it, and how to do it. In this case, the software is *Works*. This software allows you to work with word processing, spreadsheets, charts, databases, and communications.

Peripheral equipment includes the parts of the computer other than the central processing unit, such as the keyboard, screen or display, and printer. Peripheral equipment is a category of hardware.

The *prompt* is shown on your screen as >, preceded by the letter of the disk drive you are using at the moment. It alerts you that the computer has been booted and is waiting for further instructions, in this case *Microsoft Works*.

Commands are combinations of keystrokes you use to instruct the computer to perform certain functions.

Functions are operations performed by the computer.

Additional terms will be introduced later in this chapter.

Basic Components of the IBM PC

The IBM PC has four basic components that work together as a complete system. You should become familiar with the functions and capabilities of these components:

1. The keyboard

2. The monitor, screen, or display

3. The system unit or central processing unit (CPU)

4. The printer

Keyboard

The IBM PC keyboard looks like the keyboard of a typewriter, except that it has additional keys. You can see from Figure 1-1, that the keyboard has the standard alphabetic and numeric keys, ten special function keys (to the left of the alphabetic keys), and a ten-key pad (to the right of the alphabetic keys).

TIP: | Keyboards may vary.

Figure 1-1 IBM PC Keyboard

Let's take a few moments to locate some of the keys. You will use them often as you learn *Works*.

Notice on your machine that the special-function keys are shaded darker than the alphabetic and numeric keys. These keys, known as the F-keys, make the system perform particular commands and eliminate the need to press several keys to execute these commands. Some function key commands are listed in Appendix A at the back of this manual.

To the right of the F-keys are additional special-function keys. Take a few moments to locate the following keys:

■ The *Escape* key, abbreviated ESC, is used to break or cancel a command.

■ The TAB key, labeled ($\overset{|\leftarrow}{\rightarrow|}$), is located below the ESC key. When this key is pressed, the cursor moves 5 spaces to the right (word processor) or 1 cell to the right (spreadsheet and database).

■ The *Control* key (abbreviated CTRL and located below the TAB key), along with other keys, gives the computer particular instructions.

■ The *Left Shift* key, located to the left of the spacebar, is used to capitalize letters or to obtain special characters or symbols on the right side of the keyboard. The Left shift key is labeled with an outlined upward arrow (⇑).

■ The ALT key, located below the Left Shift key, is used in *Works* to select commands. ALT represents *Alternate*.

To the right of the regular keyboard are additional special-function keys. Locate these keys:

■ The *Backspace* key—labeled with an arrow, (←)—backspaces from right to left and deletes one character at a time.

■ The *Enter or Return* key—labeled with an arrow, (⏎)—is used to complete an instruction given to the computer or to return the cursor to the left margin.

■ The *Right Shift* key—labeled, like the Left Shift key, with an outlined upward arrow—is located to the right of the question mark/diagonal slash key. This key is used to capitalize letters or to obtain special characters or symbols on the left side of the keyboard.

■ The CAPS LOCK key is located to the right of the spacebar. It works somewhat differently from a typewriter's caps lock key and allows you to type any letter in all capitals and any number as a number *without* any specialized characters printing. For example, when CAPS LOCK is on, you can type A1B2C3D4 and so on. Also, when CAPS LOCK is on, the lower-case special symbols, such as \ , . ; ' [ ] -=, are not affected. To turn on the CAPS LOCK key, press it one time. To turn off the CAPS LOCK key, press it again.

■ The ten-key pad is to the right of the backspace key with other additional special-function keys. You can enter numbers using the ten-key pad while working with *Works* by pressing the *Number Lock* (NUM LOCK) key. However, the ten-key pad is also used for cursor movement, which will be explained in the next chapter. You can tell that the NUM LOCK key is on when it allows you to enter numbers from the numeric pad. Pressing it once turns it on; pressing it again turns it off.

■ The *PRINTSCREEN* key, labeled PRTSC/*, is used to dump to the printer whatever appears on the screen. This key is not a *Works* command but is convenient to use at times. If you press the PRTSC key, an asterisk (*) appears on the screen. However, if you hold the Left or Right Shift key and press PRTSC, the data on the screen will be dumped—that is—printed if your printer is on.

■ The *Insertion* key, labeled 0/INS, is located to the right of the Caps Lock key and turns on INSERT mode. This key is used to insert new data, and when it is used, it doesn't remove or replace anything already in the data. It is automatically turned on when you start *Works*. To turn off the Insertion key, press it once.

■ The *Delete* key, abbreviated DEL, removes or erases one character at a time from the screen when the cursor is on the character.

Monitor

The *monitor*, also called the *display* or *CRT* (cathode ray tube), looks like a television screen. The screen displays the data you key and also displays instructions for you to follow.

Twenty-four vertical lines of 80 horizontal spaces each are on the IBM PC screen.

There are at least two knobs on a screen. One knob turns on the display and adjusts the screen contrast. The other controls the screen brightness for eye comfort. You will learn more about the screen and what appears on the screen in Lesson 2.

System Unit

The *system unit* houses the *CPU* (central processing unit), the "brains" of the computer. The system unit also contains the memory unit, one or more disk drives, the power supply, and other important hardware. The monitor usually rests on the CPU.

Memory

As its name implies, *memory* stores data or other information temporarily until you decide to save (store) it onto a disk. Your IBM PC has at least 384K of memory. This means the computer provides storage space for storing at least 393,216 characters. Note that part of this memory is taken up by *Works* itself.

Additional memory makes it easier to complete some of the advanced functions using *Works*.

Disk Drive

A disk drive can *write* (record) information onto a disk from memory and *read* (play) it back into memory.

Check to see if your unit has one or two drives. If you have two disk drives, they are usually labeled *A* and *B*. The first (left) drive is called *drive A*. Full-height drives are arranged side by side, A on the left and B on the right. Half-height drives are stacked with A on top of B.

The drive in use is known as the *logged disk drive*. For example, if the computer is reading data from drive A, then drive A is the logged disk drive. The disk inserted in that drive is the *logged disk*. The red light on the disk drive turns on when the drive is writing or reading data.

Disks

A *disk* is a magnetic recording medium. Disks for the IBM PC are often called *diskettes*, because they are compact, or floppy disks, because they are somewhat flexible. They measure 5 1/4 inches or 3 1/2 inches in diameter. The 5 1/4-inch disk can hold either 327,680 or 368,640 characters depending on which version of disk operating system (discussed below) you use. Another way of saying this is a double-sided disk can hold 320K or 360K.

The *write-protect notch* is the small square notched out on one side of the disk. It allows information to be written to the disk. On some software disks, if the notch is covered with a write-protect tab, you cannot write to the disk, but you can still read from it. This feature prevents accidental erasure of information. The drive uses the *index hole* (the tiny circle to the right of the large center hole) to locate desired data and keep track of what part of the disk is being used. The large oval hole is the recording surface.

To supplement the floppy disk drives, you may use a hard disk, made of rigid magnetic material and sealed inside its own drive to accommodate large amounts of data and permanent storage of files. A hard disk is made of rigid magnetic material compared to a floppy disk which is somewhat flexible. See Appendix B at the back of this manual for more information about hard disk (fixed) systems.

Care of Disks

Disks must be handled with extreme care to prevent damaging them and any information stored on them. Follow these seven steps to care for your disks.

1. Keep disks in their protective envelopes when they are not being used.

2. Avoid bending disks.

3. Store disks away from extreme heat and away from magnetic paper-clip holders, or any other pieces of equipment that contain magnets.

4. Insert disks into the disk drive carefully to avoid jamming them; make certain the label is toward you and the write-protect notch is at the left.

5. **Never** insert a disk into the disk drive while turning the system on or off, while printing, or while the drive is running.

6. When labeling a disk, if the label is already on the disk, write only with a felt-tipped pen.

7. Do not touch exposed recording surfaces.

Disk Operating System (DOS)

The computer's *disk operating system* abbreviated (*DOS*) manages the way in which information or data is entered or moved from the disk. *Works* requires that the DOS be loaded in your computer first. Instructions for loading the DOS are in Lesson 2.

Formatting a Disk

Before you can use a new disk, it must be formatted. *Formatting* a disk means preparing the disk to record information. You will need to format a blank disk. All your files will be saved on this blank data disk. Appendix C at the back of this manual describes procedures for formatting a disk.

Printer

The printer operates similarly to a typewriter, in that it prints data on paper, creating what is called a *hard copy*. However, a typewriter prints each character as you enter it, but a printer prints after the data is entered. A printer has some parts that are similar to a typewriter's—a platen, a paper bail, and a paper release.

■Summary■

- *Hardware* is the physical parts of the computer.
- *Software* is the programs which consist of the set of instructions to the computer.
- *Programs* tell the computer what to do, when to do it, and how to do it.
- *Peripheral equipment* includes the keyboard, screen, printer, and other attachments.
- The *Prompt* is shown on your screen as (>), preceded by the letter of the disk drive you are using at the moment.
- *Commands* are combinations of keystrokes you use to instruct the computer to perform certain functions.
- *Functions* are operations performed by the computer.
- The *ESC* key breaks or cancels a command.
- The *TAB* key moves the cursor.
- The *monitor*, also known as the *display* or *CRT*, displays data and instructions.
- The *system unit* houses the *CPU* (central processing unit).
- The *memory* stores data temporarily until it is saved onto a disk.
- *Writing* means recording information onto a disk.
- *Reading* means playing information from the disk into memory.
- The *logged disk drive* is the disk drive in use.

■ *DOS*, the disk operating system, manages the way in which data is written to and read from the disk; the DOS also performs other tasks such as printing and storage of files.

■ *Formatting* is preparing a new disk to record data.

■ A *hard copy* is the paper printout of data, program, or other information.

2

Getting Started

Introduction

What Is *Works*?

Works is a powerful software program that provides four tools in one package:

1. Word Processor

2. Spreadsheet with Charting, also called Graphics

3. Database

4. Communications

What Is Word Processing?

Word processing is a way of writing and revising. You can create a document, save it on a disk, then print it. You can then retrieve it and make changes and save and print the revised version.

What Is a Spreadsheet?

Generally, a spreadsheet is a prelude to the preparation of financial statements. However, *Works* allows the creation of the financial statements in final form. *Works* can complete calculations through the use of formulas to provide information for forecasting data, profit and loss breakdowns, investment and sales analysis, budgeting, inventory management, and many more business applications.

What Is a Chart?

Charts (graphs) come in many forms: pie charts, bar charts, 100 percent line charts, stacked-bar charts, high-low-close charts, area charts, and X-Y charts. The old saying "a picture is worth a thousand words" is as true in business reports as elsewhere. Information is more easily understood when displayed in the form of a chart. Charts are created from the information provided in a spreadsheet or a database.

What Is a Database?

A database is defined as a collection of information for a specific purpose. This collection involves finding, extracting, and sorting information. Examples might include sales reports, accounts payable and receivable, and certain personnel or customer information. These are just a few of the many uses of databases.

What Is Communications?

A communications program allows your computer to communicate with other computers. The following are some common applications:

Electronic bulletin boards, which allow you to dial in to the system to exchange messages or receive information.

Electronic banking, in which some banks allow you to dial in to the bank's computer to obtain information about your accounts or to transfer funds.

Personal dialing directories, whereby you can use your program as a personal telephone dialer. Numbers called often can be stored and, through the use of a modem that supports automatic dialing, the system can dial any of the numbers and transfer information.

Other communication activities include sending or receiving messages, transferring files or data between computers; or functioning like another computer.

Booting (DOS) Your IBM PC

Booting means to activate your computer. Here are the procedures for starting your IBM PC using a one- or two-floppy-disk system (see Appendix B for information on booting a hard disk system).

To boot the DOS, follow these steps.

1. Hold the DOS disk so its long, exposed oval points away from you and the label is facing up.

2. Slide the disk carefully all the way into Drive A, close the drive door.

3. Turn your computer on. Be sure to turn on your screen as well.

   a. The power switch on the computer is the red switch on the unit's right side. Flip it up to turn the unit on. When the computer is loading a disk, the in-use light comes on. Do not open a disk drive if the in-use light is on.

   b. The monitor has two knobs, one to turn the machine on and one to adjust contrast and brightness. If you have a color monitor, turn it on. (The monochrome monitor comes on automatically.) Using the other knob you may want to adjust contrast and brightness. Turn the knob clockwise to increase the brightness and counterclockwise to decrease the brightness and contrast.

   c. To restart the computer when it is already on, press and hold down, in this order; CRTL, ALT, DEL. Then release all three keys.

      CTRL is to the left of the letter A.

      ALT is to the left of the spacebar.

      DEL is on the bottom row of keys below the ten-key pad.

   The location of these keys is different on the new enhanced keyboard.

TIP: Use the command CTRL-ALT-DEL **only** to restart the system when the power is already on. Do not use this command to restart the system when you are making changes in data, because the changes you have made will not be saved.

4. Respond to the date and time requests, pressing ENTER after each one.
   RETURN/ENTER: The Labels ENTER and RETURN are interchangeable. RETURN or ENTER is used to complete a command or to insert carriage returns similar to those on a typewriter. When you are ready to begin a new paragraph when typing text, press ENTER. *Works* inserts a charac-

acter called a paragraph mark (¶). The text will not wordwrap (carry or wrap words to the next line if they do not fit within the right margin) when this symbol occurs.

Cursor: The blinking light on your screen is the cursor. Like the printing point on a typewriter, it marks your position and moves as you enter data.

Date: Use the month-day-year format, separating the numbers with dashes or slashes. For the number 1, use the top-row number 1. Never use the letter *l* for the number 1. Press ENTER after the date is entered. Enter the date in one of the following ways: 3/15/88 or 03/15/88 or 3-15-88 or 03-15-88

Time: Type the correct hour and minutes, with the colon. The IBM PC uses a 24-hour clock. For example, 8:10 means 8:10 a.m.; 20:10 means 8:10 p.m. Press ENTER after the time is entered.

5 The screen will show the message A> or C> if using a hard disk. (Messages may vary depending on the configuration when *Works* was installed.)

Works Educational Version Disks

This *Works* package includes one *Works Educational Version* disk. Microsoft developed this disk for educational use only and has included the commands necessary for you to begin learning *Works*. The instructions in this manual refer to the *Educational Version* disks as your program disks. The full version of the *Works* disk contains several additional commands not included in your educational version.

Loading *Works*

The computer is ready to accept any program. You must load the program disk at this time.

Follow these steps to load *Works*:

1 Remove the DOS disk from Drive A and replace it with the program disk.

2 Type Works at the DOS prompt.

3 Press ENTER. The *Works* title screen, which shows copyright information, will briefly appear; then a box will appear (called a dialog box). This box is the "New" menu from which you can select one of the 4 tools.

Selecting a Command

Commands tell *Works* what to do. You might choose a command to tell *Works* to save a file and another to tell it to print a file. Commands appear in groups or lists in dialog boxes. The lists are called *menus*. The first menu that appears is called the *New Menu*. This menu lists in a dialog box all the tools available to you—Word Processor, Spreadsheet, Database, or Communications. From this menu you select a command (in this case, a tool).

Follow these steps to select a command:

1. Make certain your program disk is in drive A. Notice that in the dialog box a dot appears with a flashing underscore under it in the parentheses beside Word Processor. When the period appears in parentheses beside a tool, pressing ENTER will select that tool.

2. Press and release the ALT key located to the left of the spacebar. The first letter in each tool name becomes bold or highlighted. You may type the letter for the tool you want to use. Each tool can be selected in this manner. The computer reads both upper- and lower-case letters. You may also select a tool by moving the up or down cursor arrow keys (located on the ten-key pad) to move the period to the desired tool.

3. Press ENTER. A *Works* area screen will appear for the tool you selected.

Reading the Word Processor *Works* Area Screen

Study your screen and Figure 2-1 as the various parts are discussed.

1. The *menu bar* lists the menu names from which you may choose depending on the tool you are using.

2. The *Ruler Line,* the scale below the menu bar, shows the margins, indents, and tab stops that are set for the document you are typing. The brackets, [and], indicate the left and right margins. Notice that they are set at 1 and 60.

3. The *selection bar* is the blank area to the left of the work area. Symbols appear in this column to indicate headers or footers, paragraphs, and automatic page breaks. The >> is the page mark and indicates the beginning of a page.

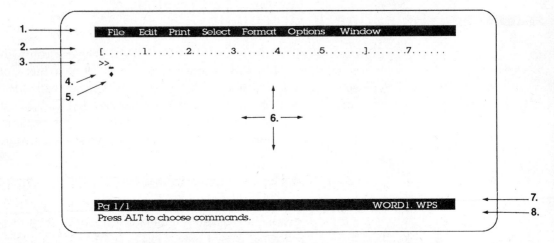

Figure 2-1 Word Processor Works Area Screen

4. The *cursor* (_) is the flashing underscore. It is your position indicator, showing you where your next typed character will appear. When you type, the cursor moves to the right.

5. The *end mark* (♦) identifies the end of a file. This symbol cannot be deleted.

6. The *work area* is the blank area of your screen where you do all your typing, editing, or formatting.

7. The *status line* shows the current page number of your document, the total number of pages, and the filename.

8. The *message line* displays messages about currently used commands.

Canceling a Command

The series of commands necessary to accomplish a function such as printing or saving a document is called a *command path*. You can cancel command path entries with the following keys:

■ BACKSPACE cancels the last entry in a command path, or backspaces to delete one character at a time.

■ ESC cancels the last entry in a command path.

Exiting *Works*

Before exiting *Works*, always make certain you have saved any information on your disk you have been working on. You will learn how to save data in Lesson 3.

To exit *Works*, follow these steps:

1. Press and release ALT. The first letter of each menu name is highlighted on the menu bar.

2. Type F (for file menu). The file menu dialog box appears.

3. Type X (for Exit).

4. Load *Works* and choose the Word Processor tool again.

Summary

To Boot DOS:

1. Hold the DOS disk so its long, exposed oval points away from you and the label is facing up.

2. Slide the disk carefully all the way into Drive A; close the drive door.

3. Turn your computer on. Be sure to turn on your screen as well.

4. Respond to the date and time requests, pressing ENTER after each one. The message A> (or C> if you are using a hard disk) will appear on your screen.

To Load Works from a Floppy Disk:

1. Remove the DOS disk from Drive A and replace it with the program disk.

2. Type Works at the DOS prompt.

3. Press ENTER. The *Works* title screen, which shows copyright information, will briefly appear; then a box will appear (called a dialog box) from which you can select one of the four tools.

To Select a Command:

1. Make certain your program disk is in Drive A.

2. Press then release the ALT key located to the left of the spacebar. The first letter in each tool name becomes bold or highlighted. You may type the bold letter for the tool you want to use. Each tool can be selected in this manner. The computer reads both upper-and lower-case letters. You may also select a tool by moving the up or down cursor arrow keys (located on the ten-key pad) to move the period to the desired tool.

3. Press ENTER. A *Works* area screen will appear for the tool you selected.

To Cancel a Command:

BACKSPACE cancels the last entry in a command path, or backspaces to delete one character at a time.

ESC cancels the last entry in a command path.

To Exit Works:

1. Press and release ALT. The first letter of each menu name is highlighted on the menu bar.

2. Type F (for file menu). The file menu dialog box appears.

3. Type X (for Exit).

3

Word Processor

Microsoft Works word processor has many features that allow you maximum flexibility in revising, correcting, and expanding your written communications. You will find it easy to type a letter or memo, but most importantly it will be easy to go back and make changes without retyping the document. Here is what you can do with the word processor:

- Make corrections.
- Add, copy, or move text.
- Use different fonts (a font is a set of characters that can be recognized as one typeface) and different sizes and styles of type (for instance, boldface).
- Insert charts and tables from the spreadsheet.
- Add headers, footers, and page numbers automatically.
- Create form letters and mailing labels and fill in forms by merging information from the database.

Since the goal of this manual is to get you off to a running start using *Works*, only the basic concepts are taught. Many of the features just listed are on your program disk, but space does not allow all of them to be covered here. Refer to *Microsoft Works Reference*.

■ *Works* Menus

To let you choose tasks (commands), *Works* displays on-screen summaries. These summaries, as mentioned earlier, are called *menus*. The menus explain the various commands available to you and highlight their first letters to give you an easy method of selection. However, if there is more than one menu name beginning with the same letter, another letter within the name is highlighted. An example is F (for File menu) and T (for Format menu). You will use these menus continually in *Works*.

You should become familiar with each menu as it is presented. Here are brief explanations of each of the seven menus you have available from the text area in the word processor. (A summary of all of the *Works* menus used most often appears in Appendix D at the back of this manual.)

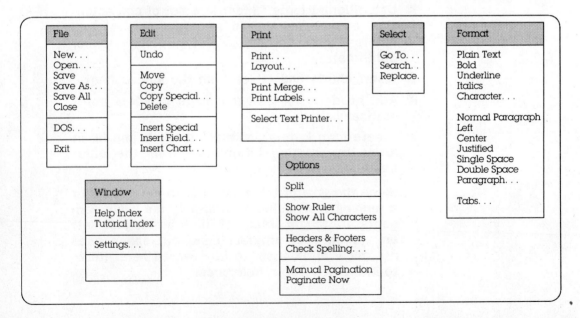

Figure 3-1 *Works* **Menus**

NOTE: The window menu shows the *Help Index* and the *Tutorial Index*. These files are not included in the educational version of the disk.

1. The *file menu* opens an existing *Works* file; saves a file; closes a file (clears the screen of the file); allows you to exit to DOS and return, or exit and quit; and allows you to view your file directory.

2. The *edit menu* allows you to copy, delete and undo deleted text, and insert text.

3. The *print menu* lets you print the current active file, select your page layout (margins, headers, footers, page numbers), merge, print labels, and select the text printer.

4. The *select menu* lets you go to a specific page in a file, or search and replace information in a file.

5. The *format menu* offers such format options as plain text, boldface, underlining, italics, and character formats which include style, position, and font. Other options include left, center and justified text, single or double spacing, control of paragraph formats, and sets and removes tab stops.

6. From the *options menu* you can create panes to view different parts of a file (split), display or hide the ruler line or special characters such as codes, display or hide headers and footers, paginate (divide into pages) manually the document, and paginate automatically.

7. The *window menu* displays settings such as for a color monitor, etc.; and the names of the documents you have opened. The Help and Tutorial Indexes are not included.

To view each menu, follow these steps:

1. Press and release ALT to highlight the letters to select a menu.

2. Type F (for file menu) and view the choices listed.

3. Press ESC when you have finished viewing.

4. Press ALT and type the highlighted letter of the menu until you have viewed all menus. Press ESC after each menu.

▰▰ Creating a Document

When you type a letter, a memo, or a report with *Works*, you use your microcomputer to create a document. This procedure is also called "opening a file." When you open a file, three important marks appear on your screen. You learned about these marks in Lesson 2, but let's review their purpose.

> \> The *page mark* identifies the beginning of a page.

> _ The *blinking underscore* is called a cursor. When you type, the text is inserted at the cursor.

> ◆ The *end mark* identifies the end of a file. This symbol cannot be deleted.

To create a document, follow these steps:

1. If you are not already in the typing area, enter *Works* and select the word processor. The typing area will appear.

2. Entering text with the word processor is similar to typing on a typewriter. Remember, you do not have to press RETURN at the end of a line because *Works* will wordwrap to the next line any words that do not fit within the margins. Don't worry about mistakes or typographical errors. You will learn how to make corrections later in this chapter. Press the TAB key (located to the left of the Q key) one time to indent the paragraph 5 spaces. *Works* has pre-set tabs every five spaces set in the program. Type this paragraph:

   The cursor is a flashing underscore that indicates your position on a page. The cursor guides you along a line while you key in text, but it can also be positioned under any character on a line so you can change the text. Now press ENTER.

3. Leave the file on your screen.

   NOTE: When CL or NL appears on the status line, the caps lock and/or num lock keys are on. To turn them off just press the proper key again.

▰▰ Cursor Movement

Now that you have typed your first document, let's learn how to move your cursor around in the text without changing anything you've typed. You can move the cursor from one position to another by using one of the IBM keyboard's arrow keys on the ten-key pad on the right side of your keyboard.

To move the cursor, complete the following procedures:

1. Press CTRL+HOME (Hold down CTRL while pressing HOME.)

2. Press the right-arrow key (—>) on the ten-key pad to move the cursor several times.

3. Press the left-arrow key (←) to move the cursor several times.

4. Press the down-arrow key (↓) several times.

5. Press the up-arrow key (↑) several times.

6. Press HOME to move the cursor to the beginning of the line.

7. Press END to move the cursor to the end of the line.

8. Press CTRL+HOME to move the cursor to the beginning of the file.

9. Press CTRL+END to move the cursor to the end of the file.

10. Press CTRL+right arrow to advance whole words at a time to the right.

11. Press CTRL+left arrow to advance whole words at a time to the left.

Scrolling

As your text fills the entire screen, *Works* moves or scrolls the text you've already typed off the top of the screen in order to show you the lines you are typing.

You can press PGUP or PGDN to move the file by "screenfuls" up or down. Even though the text cannot be seen, it is still there and will print.

Formatting

Works offers several commands that will change the looks of a document or add emphasis to certain words, phrases, or paragraphs to make documents look more professional. Here are some of the features you may choose from the format menu.

Bold	Subscript
Italics	Superscript
Underline	Plain
Strikethrough	

Some printers cannot print all of these styles. Check with your instructor before you use any one of them, or refer to your printer manual.

Let's learn how to underline, using the paragraph you created earlier.

To underline, follow these steps:

1. Position the cursor under the first character of the word *cursor* in the first sentence.

2. Press and release F8. The word EXTEND appears on the status line.

3. Tap the right-arrow key and highlight the word *cursor*. The procedure for highlighting text is called *selecting*. Here are some shortcuts when selecting text: (Do not attempt these at this time; study the procedures only.)
    Press and release F8:
        Once to select a word
        Twice to select a sentence
        Three times to select a paragraph
        Four times to select an entire file
    Press the up or down arrows to select a line at a time

4. Press and release ESC to turn off EXTEND.

5. Press and release ALT.

6. Type T (for the format menu).

7. Type U (for Underline). The text to be underlined will become highlighted on your screen. A capital U will appear on the Status Line when the cursor is under any character in the word. When the file is printed, this text will be underlined.

8. Continue to underline *cursor* each time it occurs in the file.

Files

Documents or files on the computer are similar to the files in a file drawer. In a manual system, documents, such as letters, reports, and memos, are kept in file folders and stored in the proper filing cabinets according to their label names. When you need a file, you usually request it or look for it by the name on its label. Think of *Works* as an electronic filing cabinet and each disk as a file drawer containing document files with labels or names.

Filename/Extension

Some word processing software requires that you name a file before you type it. *Works*, however, instructs you to type the document, then save and name it. You will notice an extension, such as .WPS, on your screen. You will learn more about this extension later.

Saving and Naming a File

After completing a document, you must tell the computer that you are through typing and want to save what you have done. You can save a document in three ways:

■ *Save As*. If you are working in a new file, use Save As to give the file a name and save it for the first time.

■ *Save*. If you are working in an existing file, use Save to save the file with your changes. The new version of the file replaces the original version and retains the same filename.

■ *Save All*. In *Works*, you can have up to eight files open at one time. Use Save All to save all open files. Just like Save, the new versions overwrite the old ones and retain the same filenames.

Naming A Document

Here are some rules concerning filenames and extensions:

Each document name

1. May contain 1-8 characters, but no more than 8.
2. May contain numerals or characters.
3. May not contain spaces or * ? / . " ; [ ] + =
4. May include $ & # @ ! % ( ) - { } _ ~ ^ ` '
5. May not use previous document names.
6. May not use names the system has reserved for the operation of the DOS or *Works*.
7. May be typed in upper-case or lower-case letters. When you type in lower-case, the system converts the letters to upper-case.

8. Should be selected carefully to best describe the document you are typing.

9. Precede the filename with b: when saving on a data disk.

Document Name Extensions

To help *Works* distinguish between its various tools, the extension tells the computer whether the file is a word processor, spreadsheet, database, or communications file. The filenames and their extensions might look like this:

CHAPTER5.WPS	(.WPS represents word processor files)
1QTR.WKS	(.WKS represents spreadsheet files)
EMPLOYEE.WDB	(.WDB represents database files)
PHONENOS.WCM	(.WCM represents communications files)

When you create a new file without an extension, or if you save a file without typing an extension in the filename, *Works* will automatically add the appropriate extension.

To save and name a new file on your data disk, follow these steps:

1. After you have completed the document, press and release ALT; choose the file menu; type A (for Save As).

2. The system will ask you to enter a filename. Name the file b:PRACTICE. Remember, you do not have to type the extension—*Works* will add .WPS for word processor. If another filename is shown, type over it with your new filename.

3. Press ENTER. Notice that the filename now appears on the right side of the status line.

Printing a File

Before learning how to print a file, let's review the stages your file has been through.

1. The document was first created on the screen; at that point it existed only in the computer's memory.

2. It was then saved onto a disk. You knew when this process was happening because the disk drive's red light came on.

Now you are ready to print a file. The print menu is listed on your menu bar. You will print using this menu.

To print a file, follow these steps:

1. Make certain your printer is on and loaded with paper. See your instructor if you have questions about your printer.

2. Press and release ALT; type P (for print menu). Print is now highlighted, so just press ENTER. The print dialog box will appear. The filename PRACTICE.WPS remains on your screen.

3. Your options are as follows:

   a. Number of copies (*Works* is set automatically for 1 copy.)

   b. Print specific pages (You may select certain pages of multipage documents to print.)

   c. Print to file—(This option prints the existing file you name to a file on your disk rather than to the printer.)

   d. Draft quality—(Press ALT, hold it down, press D allows you to quickly print a copy.)

   For now, don't choose any of the options.

4. Press ENTER to begin print. *Page - 1* will print at the bottom of the page.

   Many times you will not want pages numbered, for instance, in a letter.

To print without page numbers, follow these steps:

1. Press and release ALT; type P (for print menu), type L (for layout). The layout dialog box will appear.

2. Press and release ALT to highlight the selections.

3. Press ALT, hold it down and press F. Backspace to delete the footer off the line.

4. Press ENTER.

5. Press and release ALT, press P to select the print menu.

6. Press ENTER to select one copy to be printed.

7. Press ENTER to begin printing.

Closing a File

When you create a file, it remains open on your screen until you close it with the Close command from the file menu, or until you exit *Works*. Closing a file erases it from your screen; if you have saved it, it is still on your disk. If you have not saved the file, *Works* will ask you if you want to save it.

To close a file, follow these steps:

1 Press and release ALT and type F (for file menu).

2 Type C (for close). *Do not* press ENTER. The file disappears from your screen, which shows a blank typing area. If you have retrieved the file and made changes, you will get a dialogue box that asks you if you want to save the changes. Press Enter for yes or press ALT then N for no.

System Defaults

System default conditions are preset format instructions that have been programmed into *Works'* system. They save you time when you start working with a document because you do not have to set margins, tabs, line spacing, and so on, each time you begin. These conditions can be changed to suit the needs of your documents. Here is a list of *Works'* default conditions:

- Margins: 1.3 inches, left margin, 1.2 inches, right margin (60-space line), and 1 inch, top and bottom margin
- First line on each page: line 7
- Single spacing
- Ragged right margin
- Standard page length and width: 8 1/2 by 11 inches (66 lines)
- 10 pitch (pica)
- Wordwrap (When a word is too long and would exceed the right margin, the entire word is moved to the next line.)
- Automatic page numbering
- Continuous paper feed

These settings can be changed as needed.

NOTE: .. *Works* . allows . you . to . display . all . symbols . such . as . spaces . and . carriage . returns . by . using . the . *Show . All . Characters* . command . from . the . options . menu. . . If . you . see . a . para- graph . symbol . (¶) . when . you . enter . the . word . processor, . your . *Show . All . Characters* . command . is . on. . .To . turn . it . on . or . off, . select . the . command. ¶
¶

Your . copy . might . look . like . these . paragraphs . with . dots . representing . spaces . and . the . paragraph . symbols . rep- resenting . carriage . returns. ¶

Opening (Retrieving) an Existing File for Revisions

After a document has been typed and saved, it is often necessary to revise (make changes in) the document. Perhaps a report needs to be updated with current information or a paragraph added to or deleted from a letter. One of the most helpful, time-saving uses of the word processor is in revising previously keyed information. The saved document is recalled, changes are made, and the revised document is saved with the changes and printed.

To open an existing document, follow these steps:

1 Press ALT and release, type F (for file menu). Type O to select the Open command. *Works* displays the Open dialog box and shows the following:

A place for the filename to be typed
Which drive the file is in
An alphabetic list of all filenames, with extensions
Other drives and directories—drives A, B, or C.
List which files—do you want to see all *Works* files or just those created with the word processor, or the other specific tools.

2 Press and release ALT.

3 The system is asking for the filename. Type the filename b:PRACTICE.WPS

4 Press ENTER. The file appears on your screen.

■■■■■ Text Editing

One of the important skills you have to develop is the ability to edit text. *Text editing* is the process of making corrections, changes, and revisions in previously stored text. Text-editing is easy to carry out once you have a basic understanding of cursor movement, inserting text, and deleting text. With just these three features, you can efficiently alter any document.

Deleting and Inserting Text

Text may be deleted by simply backspacing; however, when several lines, paragraphs or pages are to be deleted, you must first identify the unwanted text by marking it (highlighting or extending as you did when underlining).

To delete and replace characters, words, or short phrases, follow these steps:

1 Move the cursor to the beginning character of the word *indicates* in the first sentence.

2 Press the DEL key until the word is deleted.

3 Type the new word *shows*.

4 Replace the word *key* with *type* in the second sentence.

To delete larger blocks of text, follow these steps:

1 Move the cursor to the beginning of the last sentence.

2 Press and release F8 and extend the highlight to cover the sentence.

3 Press ESC to turn off EXTEND.

4 Press and release ALT, type E (for edit menu).

5 Type D (for delete). The selected text will be deleted.

To insert new text, follow these steps:

1 Be certain the cursor is at the end of the paragraph.

2 Type this sentence: Changing text is called "text editing." The text is added to the left of the cursor. When text is added to the middle of a paragraph, *Works* adjusts lines of text to accommodate the new material.

3 Save the file by pressing and releasing ALT, type F (for file menu), type A (for Save as). The system will ask "Replace existing file?" Press ENTER for yes (OK).

4 Clear your screen. Press and release ALT; type F (for file menu); type C (for Close).

Summary

To View Each Menu:

1. Press and release ALT to highlight the letters to select a menu.

2. Type F (for file menu) and view the choices listed.

3. Press ESC when you have finished viewing.

4. Press ALT and type the highlighted letter of the menu until you have viewed all menus. Press ESC after each menu.

To Create a Document:

1. Enter *Works* and select the word processor. The typing area will appear.

2. Enter the text with the Word Processor. Remember, you do not have to press RETURN at the end of a line because *Works* will wordwrap to the next line any words that do not fit within the margins.

To Move the Cursor:

1. Press CTRL+HOME to move to the beginning of a file.

2. Press the right-arrow key to move the cursor to the right.

3. Press the left-arrow key to move the cursor to the left.

4. Press the down-arrow key to move the cursor down a line at a time.

5. Press the up-arrow key to move the cursor up a line at a time.

6. Press HOME to move the cursor to the beginning of the line.

7. Press END to move the cursor to the end of the line.

8. Press CTRL+END to move the cursor to the end of the file.

9. Press CTRL+right arrow to advance whole words at a time to the right.

10. Press CTRL+left arrow to advance whole words at a time to the left.

To Underline:

1. Position the cursor under the first character to be underlined.

2. Press and release F8. The word EXTEND appears on the status line.

3. Tap the right-arrow key and highlight the word or words to be underlined.

4. Press and release ESC to turn off EXTEND.

5. Press and release ALT.

6. Type T (for the format menu).

7. Type U (for underline). When the file is printed, this text will be underlined and a capital U will appear on the status line when the cursor is under any character in the word.

To Save and Name a New File:

1. After you have completed the document, press and release ALT; choose the file menu; type A (for Save As). Be sure to type b: before the filename when using a data disk.

2. The system will ask you to enter a filename. Type the name of the file.

3. Press ENTER.

To Print a File:

1. Make certain your printer is on and loaded with paper.

2. Press and release ALT; type P (for print menu). Print is now highlighted, so just press ENTER. The print dialog box will appear.

3. Select any of the available options.

    a. Number of copies (*Works* is set automatically for 1 copy.)

    b. Print specific pages (You may select certain pages of multipage documents to print.)

    c. Print to file (This option prints the existing file you name to a file on your disk rather than to the printer.)

    d. Draft Quality (Press ALT, hold it down and press D allows you to quickly print a copy.)

4. Press ENTER to begin print. The words Page - 1 will print at the bottom of the page.

To Print Without Page Numbers:

1. Press and release ALT; type P (for print menu), choose layout. The layout dialog box will appear.

2. Press and release ALT to highlight the selections.

3. Press ALT, hold it down, and press F. Backspace to delete the footer off the line.

4. Press ENTER.

5. Press and release ALT, press P to select the print menu.

6. Press ENTER (to select 1 copy to be printed).

7. Press ENTER to begin printing.

To Close a File:

1. Press and release ALT.

2. Type F (for file menu).

3. Type C (for close). *Do not* press ENTER. The file disappears from your screen and shows a blank typing area if you have not changed the file. If changes have been made, you will see a dialog box asking you if you want to save the changes. Press Enter for yes; press Alt, then N for no.

To Open an Existing Document:

1. From the file menu, choose the Open command. *Works* displays the Open dialog box and shows the following:
   A place for the filename to be typed
   Drive the file is in—A or B and the directory name
   Alphabetic list of all filenames with extensions
   Other drives and directories—copies of backup files, drives A, B, or C.
   List which files—do you want to see all *Works'* files or just those created with the word processor, or the other specific tools.

2. Press and release ALT.

3. Type the filename preceded by b:

4. Press ENTER. The file appears on your screen.

To Delete and Replace Characters:

1. Move the cursor to the beginning character to be deleted.

2. Press the DEL key until the word is deleted.

3. Type the new word.

To Delete Larger Blocks of Text:

1. Move the cursor to the beginning of the text to be deleted.

2. Press and release F8 and extend the highlight to cover text to be deleted.

3. Press ESC to turn off EXTEND.

4. Press and release ALT; type E (for edit menu).

5. Type D (for Delete). The selected text will be deleted.

To Insert New Text:

1. Move the cursor to the position where the new text is to be inserted.

2. Type the new text. The text is added to the left of the cursor. When text is added to the middle of a paragraph, *Works* adjusts lines of text to accommodate the new material.

4

Spreadsheet

Another name for a spreadsheet is a worksheet. Worksheets are commonly used in bookkeeping or accounting; however, any information that can be listed on a page in rows and columns can be set up as a spreadsheet. Study the following example of a spreadsheet, which shows merit raises for four employees.

	File	Edit	Print	Select	Format	Options	Chart	Window		
		A		B		C		D	E	F
1					MERIT RAISES					
2					1988-1989					
3										
4						Annual		Merit		
5		Name		Employee No.		Salary		Increase		
6										
7		Judy Cox		221889		32000		2500		
8		Dale May		22342		29500		4300		
9		Ruth Hill		212336		48600		1500		
10		Lee Jones		32444		39300		3100		
11										
12										
13										
14										
15										
16										
17										
18										
19										
20										

A13

Press ALT to choose commands.   SHEET1.WKS

Figure 4-1

Do the steps with squares

In this lesson you will learn how to create, save, retrieve, edit, and print a spreadsheet. As you are learning, additional helpful information will be offered to expand your knowledge of *Works*. For instance, you will learn how to "copy" your keystrokes to help automate part of the process. Remember, our goal in this text is to get you off to a quick start.

Now that you have completed the exercises using the Word Processor, you have become familiar with the use of the ALT key in commands. It is often pressed and released or held down and another key pressed at the same time. For the remainder of this manual the commands will be shown in this manner:

Press ALT—press and release ALT

Press ALT+P—press ALT, hold it down, and press P

Press ALT, C, C—press and release ALT, press and release C, press and release C again

When commands appear at the end of a step, these are hints to help you remember the procedure. An example might be:

1. From the format menu choose the Width command (ALT, T, W).

Steps in Creating a Simple Spreadsheet

You should always plan your spreadsheet, identifying column headings, and so on, before you begin entering information in the computer. Before you begin, review these steps in building a spreadsheet:

1. Plan your spreadsheet.

2. Enter *Works* to display the blank spreadsheet.

3. Enter headings (labels).

4. Enter side headings (labels), numerical data, and formulas as needed into cells.

5. Name and save the file to the disk.

6. Print the file.

An empty spreadsheet consists of a grid or matrix of cells. A *cell* is identified by its column and row. An example is B3 (B is the column, 3 is the row). A cell may contain three types of data:

■ *Formula*. A formula is an equation used to obtain the results of a calculation, such as adding a row across or down. An example of a formula is =SUM(D1:D5). This formula means that cells D1, D2, D3, D4, and D5 are to be added. Formulas are made up of numbers; math operators, such as the + or - signs; and functions.

Another example formula is SQRT(144), which signals *Works* to figure the square root of 144 (which is 12). This formula triggers a built-in function or equation that will solve sometimes very difficult math problems. *Works* has many built-in functions from which you may choose when entering formulas.

■ *Text*. Text is any character entered that isn't interpreted by *Works* as a formula, number, date, or time. You can enter a quotation mark (") before an entry to prevent *Works* from thinking what you enter is a formula.

■ *Numbers*. A number expresses a quantity. You can enter numbers as integers (such as 887 or -887), as decimal fractions (8.87 or 0.887 or -8.7), or as fractions (1/2).

Numbers are sometimes defined as *ranges* such as A1:H9. In this example, the range begins at A1 and includes everything across to column H down to row 9. The colon separates the beginning and ending of the range.

Selecting the Spreadsheet

The procedure for selecting the *Works* spreadsheet is the same as for selecting the word processor.

To select the spreadsheet, follow these steps:

1   Make certain your program disk is in Drive A.

TIP: If you have exited *Works*, type Works at the DOS prompt.

2 Press ALT, and type S (for spreadsheet).

3 Press ENTER. A blank spreadsheet will appear on your screen.

Reading the Screen

Study your screen as the various parts are discussed.

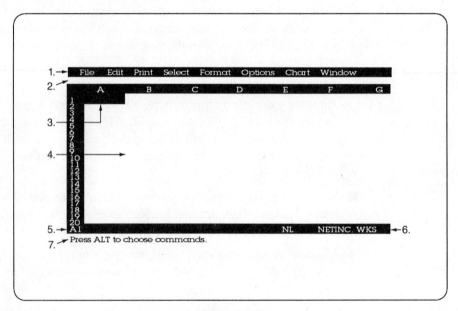

Figure 4-2

1. The *menu bar* displays eight menus that contain commands you'll use to create and organize your spreadsheet.

2. The *formula bar* is the place where information typed in the spreadsheet first appears.

3. *Cells* are what make up the work area. Cells are arranged in columns and rows. Letters across the top border identify the columns (A-G) and numbers on the left border identify the rows (1-20). The active cell (meaning the one in which you can currently enter data) is marked with a rectangular highlight.

4. The *work area* is the blank area where you'll build your spreadsheet.

5. The *reference* for each cell is determined by where its row and column meet, such as cell A5 (column A, row 5). The reference for the active cell is shown in the status line below the row numbers at the left. When you're starting out, the reference on your screen should be A1.

6. The *status line* identifies the cell reference (A1, for instance) and the name of the current file.

7. The *message line* shows suggestions and brief discussions of the commands.

Menus

Eight menus are available to you in the work area. Many of the commands are the same ones that you learned using the word processor. Figure 4-3 shows these menus.

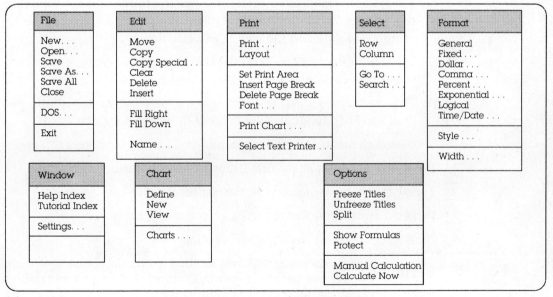

Figure 4-3

You should become familiar with each menu as it is presented. Study Figure 4-3 as you read the following.

1. The *file menu* creates new files, opens existing files, and saves and closes files, and exits to DOS temporarily or exits from the program permanently.

2. The *edit menu* performs some of the same functions as in the word processor—copies, moves, deletes, and inserts data. Some additional commands are the Fill Right and Fill Down commands. These commands copy the left-most column and top row of a sheet into the adjacent selected cells either to the right or down.

3. The *print menu* offers selections for the layout and printing of the spreadsheet and/or chart.

4. The *select menu* performs the same commands as in the word processor. You can go to or search a row or column.

5. The *format menu* provides eight commands for formatting your spreadsheet. Among the choices are setting the number of decimal places, inserting dollar signs, and identifying cells to show percentage, exponential, or true/false values. The Style command changes your spreadsheet appearance to the way it will look when it prints. The Width command is used to widen columns.

6. The *options menu* lets you freeze and unfreeze titles, show formulas, protect cells, and complete calculations. It also lets you change the appearance of data and the way it will calculate.

7. The *chart menu* lets you enter the chart screen and create a chart; lets you view a chart; and names, deletes, and copies existing charts.

8. The *window menu* controls settings and lists the names of all open files. The Help Index and the Tutorial Index are not included.

To view each menu, follow these steps:

1 Press ALT to highlight the first letters to select a menu.

2 Type F (for file menu) and view the choices listed.

3 Press the right-arrow key to view each remaining menu.

4 Press ESC when you have finished viewing.

TIP: When you press ALT and the first letters do not become highlighted, you began a command before pressing ALT and did not complete the steps. Press ESC several times to cancel the command; then press ALT again. The first letters will become highlighted.

Cursor Movement

The rectangular highlight on the active cell represents your cursor. The cursor is moved around on your spreadsheet using the arrow keys located on the ten-key pad. These arrow keys move the cursor down a line, up a line, or right and left a cell; PgDn and PgUp scroll the pages; HOME moves the cursor to column A of the current line; and END moves the cursor to the end of the current line.

To practice moving the cursor, follow these steps:

1. Your cursor should be on A1. If it is not, use the arrow-up and arrow-left keys to move it to that position.

2. Move the cursor to A2 (press the down arrow once).

3. Move the cursor to B5.

4. Move the cursor to H20. (Notice that you can move the cursor beyond the screen to H and the screen will show columns B-H. We'll say more about this shortly.)

5. Move the cursor to A1 (CTRL+HOME).

The GoTo Command

You can use the GoTo command to move the cursor to an active cell. The GoTo command is on the select menu and selects a cell or range whose reference or name you type in the dialog box. This command can be used to move to a specific location in the spreadsheet. A quick way to choose the GoTo command is to press F5.

To use the GoTo command, follow these steps:

1. Press F5.

2. Type the reference location B15.

3. Press ENTER.

4. Use GoTo again to move the active cell back to A1.

Canceling a Command

Use the ESC key to cancel commands, just as you did when using the word processor.

Erasing a Cell

Should you type text or enter data incorrectly, *Works* allows you to erase information in a cell in two ways—by clearing the cell or by deleting rows or columns of cells. Once information has been cleared or deleted, it cannot be recovered.

To use the Clear command, follow these steps:

1 Go to cell D1.

2 Type your first name on the formula line and press ENTER. Your name will appear in cell D1. Leave your cursor in cell D1.

3 From the edit menu, choose the Clear command (ALT, E, E). If you choose the Clear command by using the down arrow, you will have to press EN-TER. The cell will be cleared, and your name will be erased.

Scrolling

As you saw earlier, your screen may not show all of your spreadsheet's columns at once. *Works* uses your screen display as a window through which you can view any area of your spreadsheet. At any one time, though, you may only be viewing part of the matrix available to you. The program default is a global (meaning all) column width of 10 characters and lets you see 8 columns at a time; however, you can change the column width to any size from 0 to 79 characters.

When your spreadsheet is bigger than your computer screen, you can scroll or move your window horizontally or vertically (using the arrow keys) to different parts of the spreadsheet.

To practice scrolling horizontally, follow these steps:

1 Move the cursor to A1. Cell A1 will be highlighted.

2 Tap the right arrow until you have moved the cursor to column H. The screen now displays columns B-H.

3 Move your cursor farther to the right by holding down the right arrow. Your computer has a built-in repeat feature that causes the display to continue scrolling to the letters AF.

4 Scroll back to A1 using HOME or the left arrow.

Locks

After locking cells, all cells are locked until you unlock them. Locking means protecting the information in the cell from being changed. To lock and unlock cells, choose the Protect command from the options menu.

Typing Text (Labels)

Spreadsheets are more easily understood when labeled with headings. Some examples are Income Statement, Balance Sheet, and Expenses. *Works* allows you to enter "text" to create labels. Here is the finished spreadsheet you will create.

```
1987 EXPENSES JOHN HILL, 1182 HILL STREET, DALLAS, TX 75222
```

Months	Hse. Pmt.	Food	Util.	Phone	Gasoline	US Cr. Cd.	Total
January	455	380	151	42	89	66	1183
February	455	410	148	39	92	66	1210
March	455	370	125	33	88	66	1137
April	455	390	90	37	89	66	1127
Total	1820	1550	514	151	358	264	4657
% of Total	0.39080953403	0.3328322955	0.11037148379	0.032424307494	0.076873523728	0.056688855486	1

Figure 4-4

NOTE: Any time you make an entry that could be interpreted as a formula, it should be specified as text by preceding it with the quotation mark ("); otherwise, the system will automatically add the quotation marks for you when you type alphabetic characters.

To create a heading (label), follow these steps:

[1] Place the cell cursor in cell A1. A1 will be highlighted.

[2] Type 1987 EXPENSES JOHN HILL Type the label exactly as you want it to appear. Backspace if you make an error. CAPS LOCK locks the alphabetic keyboard on all caps yet allows the use of the numeric top row. Remember to turn CAPS LOCK off when you've finished.

[3] Press ENTER. Text will spill over into empty cells. Each cell contains 10 characters.

[4] Move the cursor to B3.

[5] Type Hse.Pmt. (Do not press ENTER).

[6] Press the right-arrow key. This enters Hse.Pmt. into cell B3 and moves the cursor to the right one column.

[7] Enter the remaining column headings and press the right arrow after each entry.

In C3 enter	Util.	(right arrow)
In D3 enter	Phone	(right arrow)
In E3 enter	Gasoline	(right arrow)
In F3 enter	Groceries	(right arrow)
In G3 enter	US Cr.Cd.	(right arrow)
In H3 enter	Total	(right arrow)

[8] Press F5 to go to cell A4.

Entering Numbers and Formulas

You are now ready to enter the first numerical data onto your spreadsheet. You may enter numbers from either the ten-key pad (by pressing the NUM LOCK key) or from the numeric keys at the top of your keyboard. Remember to turn the NUM LOCK key off when you are finished.

To enter numbers and formulas, follow these steps:

[1] Go to A4 if you are not already there.

[2] Type Jan

[3] Press the right arrow to move to the right one column to B4.

[4] Enter the expenses for the house payment. Type 455. Enter the figure as a whole number without a dollar sign (nor should you use commas in larger numbers).

5 Press the right arrow. Your column headings and amounts will not be aligned. You will learn how to align columns later in this lesson.

6 Enter the amounts for the remaining expenses:

Enter for Util.:	151	(right arrow)
Enter for Phone:	42	(right arrow)
Enter for Gasoline:	89	(right arrow)
Enter for Groceries:	380	(right arrow)
Enter for US Cr. Cd.:	66	(right arrow)

7 Enter a formula to tell *Works* to total all expenses for the month of January and place the answer in cell H4. Type =SUM(B4:G4). This formula totals all the cells you specified in a certain range (the range was from B4 to G4). As mentioned earlier, to indicate a certain range, type the first cell location, a colon as a divider, and the last cell location. Always precede a formula with an equals sign.

8 Press ENTER. The total (1183) is automatically placed in H4, indicating the total for the month of January. Move your cursor to A1. Your screen should look something like this:

```
 File   Edit   Print   Select   Format   Options   Chart   Window
 '1987 EXPENSES JOHN HILL
      A         B        C         D         E         F         G
  1  1987 EXPENSES JOHN HILL
  2
  3            Hse. Pmt  Util.      Phone    Gasoline  Groceries  US Cr. Cd.
  4    Jan       455     151         42         89        380         66
  5
  6
  7
  8
  9
 10
 11
 12
 13
 14
 15
 16
 17
 18
 19
 20
 A1
 Press ALT to choose commands.                              SHEET1.WKS
```

Figure 4-5

9 Enter the rest of the data shown below. Enter the formula in column H for each month. Leave the spreadsheet on your screen.

	A	B	C	D	E	F	G	H
1	1987 EXPENSES JOHN HILL							
2								
3		Hse.Pmt.	Util.	Phone	Gasoline	Groceries	US Cr.Cd.	Total
4	Jan	455	151	42	89	380	66	1183
5	Feb	455	148	39	92	410	66	1210
6	Mar	455	125	33	88	370	66	1137
7	Apr	455	90	37	89	390	66	1127
8								

No dollar signs

Figure 4-6

TIP: *Works* will automatically insert dollar signs, commas, and decimals for you. To use this feature, press F8 and highlight the columns and rows you will be using. Press ESC to turn off EXTEND. From the Format Menu, choose the dollar feature (Alt, T, D, press Enter). You can show decimal places as percents using this feature as well—just choose percent instead of D (Dollars).

Aligning Columns

You probably have noticed that numbers are aligned to the right under your column headings, but your column headings are not aligned over the columns. Let's learn how to align the columns.

To align columns to the right, follow these steps:

1 Go to A3, press F8 (EXTEND appears on the status line), and highlight A3 through H12 with the right and down arrows.

2 Press ALT, T (for format menu), S (for style), and press the down arrow until the dot is beside the word right.

3 Press ENTER. The columns will align to the *right*.

4 Press ESC to remove highlighting.

Adjusting the Column Width

The Width command from the format menu changes the width of all selected columns. Often information in a cell will be wider than the default width of 10 spaces. If extend is used, once the width is set, all cells in the chosen column will be set at the new width. To adjust all columns, select an entire row before setting the column width. The Width command affects all columns in the selection. You may widen the columns from 0 to 79 characters.

When a column is too narrow, the system prompts you by displaying ######. When you widen the column, the ###### will disappear. You can widen just the one column if necessary.

To widen all columns, follow these steps:

1 Select a cell in each column in the same row you want to change. Go to cell A3. Press F8 and use the arrow keys to extend the highlight to H1.

2 From the format menu choose the Width command (ALT, T, W).

3 Type the column width in the dialog box. Type 15.

4 Press ENTER. The columns will widen to 15 spaces each.

5 Press ESC to remove the highlighting.

Using the Copy Feature to Repeat Formulas

In the previous example, you entered the formula under total (column H) each time. Now you will learn a shortcut. We noted earlier that *Works* has a Fill Right command that can duplicate cell descriptions into other positions. Fill Right duplicates cell contents from one position into the next cells to the right of that position. The source copied from remains intact.

There are four features to the copy function:

■ *Fill Down* copies the top row of selected cells to the selected cells immediately below.

■ *Fill Right* copies the left-most column of selected cells into the selected cells immediately to the right (as many cells as you select).

■ *Copy* makes one copy of selected cells.

■ *Copy Special* completes three operations: it adds the selected cells to other spreadsheets; subtracts the selected cells from other spreadsheet cells; and converts a formula to its value.

In the spreadsheet on your screen, you are ready to obtain a total for the various expenses. Each formula used to total each column will be the same. Instead of typing the formula over and over on the formula bar into each cell, enter the formula in the first desired cell then use the Copy command to copy it into each cell.

To use the copy feature, follow these steps:

1 Go to cell A9. Type Total.

2 Press the right arrow to move the cursor one column to the right.

3 Enter the formula to add B4 through B7 into cell B9. Type =SUM(B4:B7)

4 Press ENTER. The total (1820) for the Hse.Pmt. column appears.

5 Press F8 and select (highlight) cells B9 through H9.

6 From the edit menu, choose the Fill Right command, because you want *Works* to total all columns to the right of B9 using the same formula you entered in cell B9 (ALT, E, R).

7 Totals should appear under each column you selected.

8 Press ESC to cancel the highlighting.

9 Go to cell A9.

Press HOME to move the cursor to A9; your screen should look something like Figure 4-7. Move the cursor to J1 to view the remainder of the spreadsheet.

File   Edit   Print   Select   Format   Options   Chart   Window
'Total

	A	B	C	D	E
1	1987 EXPENSES JOHN HILL				
2					
3		Hse. Pmt.	Util.	Phone	Gasoline
4	Jan	455	151	42	89
5	Feb	455	148	39	92
6	Mar	455	125	33	88
7	Apr	455	90	37	89
8					
9	Total	1820	514	151	358
10					
11					
12					
13					
14					
15					
16					
17					
18					
19					
20					

A9
Press ALT to choose commands.   SSHEET1.WKS

File   Edit   Print   Select   Format   Options   Chart   Window

	F	G	H	I	J
1					
2					
3	Groceries	US Cr. Cd.	Total		
4	380	66	1183		
5	410	66	1210		
6	370	66	1137		
7	390	66	1127		
8					
9	1550	264	4657		
10					
11					
12					
13					
14					
15					
16					
17					
18					
19					
20					

F9
Press ALT to choose commands.   SSHEET1.WKS

Figure 4-7

Saving a File

Works saves spreadsheets the same way it saves word processor files.

To save a file, follow these steps:

1 After you have completed the document, press ALT; choose the file menu; type A (for Save As).

2 The system will prompt you to enter a filename. Name the file b:SSHEET1 (without any spacing or punctuation).

3 Press ENTER.

Printing Your Spreadsheet

Printing your spreadsheet is much the same as printing using the word processor. The default page width is 80 characters, and the default page length is 66 lines. If your spreadsheet exceeds the page width, *Works* prints as many spreadsheet columns as it can on the first page then prints the remaining columns on a second page.

To print your spreadsheet, follow these steps:

1 Press and release ALT, type P (for print menu); type P (for print).

2 The system asks you how many copies you want. The default is one. Press ENTER to print one copy.

3 Clear the file from your screen (ALT, F, C).

NOTE: You may print only selected portions of your spreadsheet by choosing the Set Print Area command from the print menu. You would select the portion of your spreadsheet you want printed.

Opening (Retrieving) a File

Spreadsheet files are retrieved following the same procedures you learned while using the word processor.

To open a spreadsheet file, follow these steps:

1 Press ALT, choose the file menu, type O (for Open).

correct drive

2 Type the name of the file you want to retrieve. Type b:SSHEET1.WKS (without any spacing). Remember, you must type the exact name of the file. *Works* reads either upper- or lower-case letters.

3 Press ENTER.

Adding Additional Text

After completing a spreadsheet, it is often desirable to make changes to update information. Text can be added or deleted or other changes can be made. Let's add some information.

To add additional text, follow these steps:

1 Move to A3 and type the label Months

2 Press ENTER.

3 Move the cursor to cell A12 and type % of Total

4 Press ENTER.

Editing a Cell's Contents

By backspacing, you can edit data on the forumla bar before sending it to a cell, and you have seen that data in a cell can be erased by erasing the cell. *Works* provides an easy way to edit data already in a cell by using F2; however, when you are correcting, choose the most efficient method.

To edit a cell's contents, follow these steps:

1 Place your cursor in the cell to be edited. Suppose you want to change Groceries to Food. Go to cell F3.

2 Press F2. *Works* brings the entry in cell F3 to the formula line.

3 Press HOME to move the cursor to the beginning of the entry on the formula bar.

4 Press the delete key 10 times to delete "Groceries.

5 Type Food

6 Press ENTER. The new entry replaces the old one in cell F3. Notice the system added the quotation marks before food on the Formula bar when you pressed ENTER.

▬▬▬ Inserting Data

Continue learning how to make changes in your spreadsheet by inserting data.

To insert data, follow these steps:

1 Move the cursor to A1.

2 Press F2. The cursor is flashing at the end of the entry on the formula bar. Type , 1182 HILL STREET, DALLAS, TX 75222. The text must be preceded by a quotation mark (") or it cannot be edited. The system should have already added it before 1987. If no quotation mark appears, backspace the entire entry and type a " and the entry as edited.

3 Press ENTER.

4 Move the cursor to the cell to be edited. Go to cell A4.

5 Press F2. Again, *Works* brings the entry in cell A4 to the formula bar.

6 Notice that the cursor is one space after the "n" in Jan. Press HOME to move the cursor to the beginning of the entry line. Type a quotation mark (") and move the cursor one space after the "n". Type uary (to spell January in full).

7 Press the down arrow.

8 Edit the remaining months by spelling each month in full. After typing a month, press the down arrow, then repeat steps 5-7.

9 Right align the labels in cells A5 through A9. See page 46 to review procedures.

▬▬▬ Creating a Formula

You have entered the formulas for totaling columns down and across your spreadsheet. The screen now displays the results of those calculations, but how can the totals be used to determine what percentage of total expenses is in each of the categories? The formula needed can be stated in a simple way: What fraction of total expenses (100%) is the house payment to date? When we insert the information from the cells that contain the figures from our spreadsheet, the formula would read as follows: What fraction of H9 is B9? B9 divided by H9 will give us the percent.

Works has identified certain symbols on the keyboard to represent specific math functions. For instance, the slash symbol (/) means divide; therefore, our formula would now read: B9/H9 (or 1820 divided by 4657). If an equals sign (=) is placed before the formula, *Works* will recognize it as a formula: =B9/H9.

To enter the formula for computing percentages, follow these steps:

1 Move the cursor to cell B12.

2 Enter =B9/H9

3 Press the right-arrow key. Works shows 11 decimal places in the answer (.39080953403 [or 39%] appears in B12).

4 Move the cursor to cell C12 if it is not already there.

5 Enter =C9/H9

6 Press the right-arrow key [.11037148379 (or 11%) appears in C12].

7 Move the cursor to cell D12 if it is not already there.

8 Enter the remaining formulas for line 12 ending with the formula H9/H9 (the total of the percentages should equal 1 or 100%).

9 Press the right-arrow key.

10 Save and print one copy of the file.

11 Leave the file on your screen.

Your screen should look something like Figure 4-8.

TIP: Your answers can be shown as percents by selecting the row (12) from the Format Menu, choose P (for percent) and press Enter.

The Show Formulas Command

You have entered several formulas onto your spreadsheet. *Works* displayed each total or percent decimal in the proper cell.

Up to this point, to know what formula was entered in any one cell you could view the formula only from the formula bar by moving the cursor to the desired cell, and you could read only one formula at a time. When working with formulas, it is often helpful to view them all at once. *Works* provides a global command (Show Formulas) that allows you to view the formulas entered in each cell. The results of the formulas' calculations

```
     File  Edit  Print  Select  Format  Options  Chart  Window
"% of Total
           A              B             C              D               E
1   1987 EXPENSES JOHN HILL, 1182 HILL STREET, DALLAS TX 75222
2
3        Months        Hse. Pmt       Util.          Phone           Gasoline
4        January          455          151            42               89
5        February         455          148            39               92
6        March            455          125            33               88
7        April            455           90            37               89
8
9        Total           1820          514           151              358
10
11
12     % of Total   0.39080953403  0.11037148379  0.032424307494  0.076873523728
13
14
15
16
17
18
19
20
A12
Press ALT to choose commands.                              SSHEET1.WKS
```

```
     File  Edit  Print  Select  Format  Options  Chart  Window
=F9/H9
           F                  G              H             I            J
1
2
3         Food            US Cr. Cd.        Total
4         380                66            1183
5         410                66            1210
6         370                66            1137
7         390                66            1127
8
9        1550               264            4657
10
11
12    0.33283229547    0.056688855486                    1
13
14
15
16
17
18
19
20
F12
Press ALT to choose commands.                              SSHEET1.WKS
```

Figure 4-8

will temporarily be replaced with the formulas themselves. When you repeat the command, the results will reappear.

To display formulas with the Show Formulas command, follow these steps:

1. Move the cursor to B12.

2. From the options menu, choose the Show Formulas command (ALT, O, F)

3. Press the right-arrow key to view the formulas in each column.

4. Repeat step 2 to return to the formulas' calculations.

Operators and Formulas

Works provides several useful mathematical functions that are built into the system. These functions allow you to perform calculations quickly between a range of cells. For example, earlier in this text, instead of referring to each cell location, you used the formula =SUM(B4:B7)—the = identifying it as a formula for *Works*, SUM meaning to add, and B4 and B7 specifying the range from cell B4 to cell B7 to be added.

Certain symbols on your keyboard have been designated to do arithmetic calculations when using *Works*. They are called operator keys. Here are some examples of math problems and how *Works* would read these functions to complete the calculations:

Arithmetic Function	Example	Answer	Explanation	Works' Operator Key
Addition	333+222	555	Adds	+
Subtraction	333-111	222	Subtracts	-
Multiplication	12*12	144	Multiplies	*
Division	144/12	12	Divides	/

For our example, we created one formula—=B9/H9—and used one built-in formula— =SUM(B4:B7). *Works* has created many formulas from which you may choose. Refer to the *Works'* manual for a complete list of these formulas. Here are a few statistical functions:

AVG(Range Reference 1, Range Reference 2, . . .)
Averages the values of all items in a range.
COUNT(Range Reference 1, Range Reference 2, . . .)
Counts the number of all items in a range.

MAX(Range Reference 1, Range Reference 2, . . .)
  Finds the maximum value of all items in a range.
MIN(Range Reference 1, Range Reference 2, . . .)
  Finds the minimum value of all items in a range.
SUM(Range Reference 1, Range Reference 2, . . .)
  Adds the values of all items in a range.

Inserting, Deleting, and Moving Rows and Columns

You have learned many of the important commands such as Save, Load, Open, Close, and Print. Other commands allow you to add columns and rows with the Insert command or to remove them with the Delete command. Rows and columns can also be repositioned by using the Move command.

To insert a column, follow these steps:

|1| Move the cursor to E3.

|2| You want to insert a column between D and E. To select column E, press ALT, S, C.

|3| From the edit menu, choose the Insert command (ALT, E, I).

|4| A blank column will appear between D and E and all information will move one column to the right.

|5| Press ESC to cancel the highlighting.

TIP: Should a dialog box appear saying "too many columns" when you are widening your columns, you may have entered a space or other character somewhere to the right of your spreadsheet. Highlight (F8) all the blank area to the right of your spreadsheet and press Alt, E (Edit), D (Delete) to delete any information you might have accidentally entered.

You have added a new column between D and E. Now you will delete the column you added.

To delete (erase) a column, follow these steps:

|1| Be certain cursor is in column E. To select column E, press ALT, S, C. Column E will become highlighted.

[2] From the edit menu, choose the Delete command (ALT, E, D). You do not have to press ENTER. The column will automatically be deleted when you type D. Press ESC to remove the highlight.

Another helpful command is the Move command. This command allows you to move data to avoid reentering it. In the following practice, you will move Food to Column C.

To move a column, follow these steps:

[1] Be certain cursor is in column F. To select column F, press ALT, S, C.

[2] From the edit menu, choose the Move command (ALT, E, M).

[3] Position your cursor at column C to select where you want the column to be moved (ALT, S, C).

[4] Press ENTER. The Food column is moved to column C. Press ESC to cancel the highlight.

Save and print a copy of the file.

Your copy should look something like Figure 4-9:

1987 EXPENSES JOHN HILL, 1182 HILL STREET, DALLAS, TX 75222

Months	Hse. Pmt.	Food	Util.	Phone	Gasoline	US Cr. Cd.	Total
January	455	380	151	42	89	66	1183
February	455	410	148	39	92	66	1210
March	455	370	125	33	88	66	1137
April	455	390	90	37	89	66	1127
Total	1820	1550	514	151	358	264	4657
% of Total	0.39080953403	0.33283229547	0.11037148379	0.032424307494	0.076873523728	0.056688855486	1

Figure 4-9

Formatting a Spreadsheet

You used the format menu earlier when you expanded the columns to 15 spaces (Width command). Another useful command from the format menu is the Style command. Here are some of its functions:

■ *Alignment.* The default alignment is left alignment for text and right alignment for numbers. You used this earlier in this lesson to create right alignment for columns.

■ *Bold, Underline, Italics.* The cells are selected; then using the Style command; bold, underline, or italics is chosen. It will be highlighted on the screen.

■ *Locked.* This function prevents the contents of a cell from being changed.

To view the Style command, follow these steps:

1 From the format menu, select the Style command (ALT, T, S).

2 Press ALT. The first letters become highlighted.

3 When you are finished, press ESC to return to your screen.

Summary

To Select the Spreadsheet:

1. Make certain your program disk is in Drive A.

2. Press ALT and type S (for spreadsheet).

3. Press ENTER. A blank spreadsheet will appear on your screen.

To View Each Menu:

1. Press ALT to highlight the first letters to select a menu.

2. Type F (for file menu) and view the choices listed.

3. Press the right-arrow key to view each remaining menu.

4. Press ESC when you have finished viewing.

To Move the Cursor

The arrow keys move the cursor up a line, down a line, or left and right a cell; PGUP and PGDN scroll the pages; HOME moves the cursor to column A of the current line; and END moves the cursor to the end of the current line.

To Use the GoTo Command:

1. Press F5.

2. Type the reference location.

3. Press ENTER.

To Use the Clear Command:

From the edit menu, choose the clear Command (ALT, E, E). If you choose the Clear command by using the down arrow, you will have to press EN-TER. The cell will be cleared.

To Practice Scrolling Horizontally:

1. Move the cursor to A1. Cell A1 will be highlighted.

2. Tap the right arrow until you have moved the cursor to column H. The screen now displays columns B-H.

3. Move your cursor farther to the right by holding down the right arrow. Your computer has a built-in repeat feature that causes the display to continue scrolling to the letters AF.

4. Scroll back to A1 using HOME or the left arrow.

To Create a Heading (Label):

1. Place the cell cursor in the cell where the label is to go.

2. Type the label exactly as you want it to appear. Backspace if you make an error. CAPS LOCK locks the alphabetic keyboard on all caps yet allows the use of the numeric top row. Remember to turn CAPS LOCK off when you've finished.

3. Press ENTER. Text may spill over into empty cells. Each cell contains 10 characters.

To Enter Numbers and Formulas:

1. Go to the cell where the number or formula is to be entered.

2. Enter the figures as whole numbers without dollar signs or commas. Always precede a formula with an equals sign. Formulas cause the results of their calculations to automatically appear in cells.

To Align Columns to the Right:

1. Press F8 (EXTEND appears on the status line) and highlight the rows to be aligned.

2. Press ALT, T (for format menu), S (for style); and press the down arrow until the dot is beside the word right.

3. Press ENTER. The columns will align to the right.

4. Press ESC to remove the highlighting.

To Widen All Columns:

1. Select a cell in each column in the same row you want to change. Press F8 and use the arrow keys to extend the highlight to the cells desired.

2. From the format menu choose the Width command (ALT, T, W).

3. Type the column width in the dialog box.

4. Press ENTER. The columns will widen.

5. Press ESC to remove the highlighting.

To Use the Copy Feature:

1. Go to the cell containing the information to be copied.

2. Press F8 and select cells to copy to.

3. From the edit menu, choose the Fill Right or Fill Down command.

4. Press ESC to cancel the highlighting.

To Save a File:

1. After you have completed the document, press ALT; choose the file menu; type A (for Save As).

2. The system will prompt you to enter a filename. Type the filename preceded by b:

3. Press ENTER.

To Print Your Spreadsheet:

1. From the print menu, choose Print (ALT, P, P).

2. The system asks you how many copies you want. The default is one. Press ENTER to print one copy.

3. Clear the file from your screen (ALT, F, C).

To Open a Spreadsheet File:

1. Press ALT, choose the file menu, type O (for Open).

2. Type the name of the file you want to retrieve preceded by b:. Remember, you must type the exact name of the file. *Works* reads either upper-or lower-case letters.

3. Press ENTER.

To Add Additional Text:

1. Move to the cell where the information is to be added.

2. Type the text to be added.

3. Press ENTER.

To Edit a Cell's Contents:

1. Place your cursor in the cell to be edited.

2. Press F2. *Works* brings the cell's entry to the formula bar.

3. Press HOME to move the cursor to the beginning of the entry on the formula bar.

4. Press the delete key until the entry is deleted.

5. Type the new entry.

6. Press ENTER. The new entry replaces the old one.

To Insert Data:

1. Move the cursor to the cell where the data is to be inserted.

2. Press F2. The cursor is flashing at the end of the formula bar. Type the information to be inserted. The text must be preceded by a quotation mark (") or it cannot be edited. The system should have added the quotation mark before the entry. If no quotation mark appears, backspace the entire entry and type a " and the entry as edited.

3. Press ENTER.

4. Align any columns needed.

To Display Formulas with the Show Formulas Command:

1. Move the cursor to a cell containing a formula.

2. From the options menu, choose the Show Formulas command (ALT, O, F).

3. Press the right arrow key to view the formulas in each column.

4. Repeat step 2 to return to the formulas' calculations.

To Insert a Column:

1. Move the cursor to where the column is to be inserted.

2. Select the column by pressing ALT, S, C.

3. From the edit menu, choose the Insert command (ALT, E, I).

4. A blank column will appear and all information will move one column to the right.

5. Press ESC to cancel the highlighting.

To Delete (Erase) a Column:

1. Be certain the cursor is at the beginning of the column to be deleted. Select the column to be deleted by pressing ALT, S, C. The column will become highlighted.

2. From the edit menu, choose the Delete command (ALT, E, D). You do not have to press ENTER. The column will automatically be deleted when you type D.

3. Press ESC to cancel the highlight.

To Move a Column:

1. Be certain the cursor is at the beginning of the column to be moved. Select the column to be moved by pressing ALT, S, C.

2. From the edit menu, choose the Move command (ALT, E, M).

3. Select the position to where you want the column to be moved. (ALT, S, C).

4. Press ENTER. The column is moved.

5. Press ESC to cancel the highlight.

To View the Style Command:

1. From the format menu, select the Style command. (ALT, T, S).

2. Press ALT. The first letters become highlighted.

3. When you are finished, press ESC to return to your screen.

5

Charting

Charting, often called graphing, helps clarify or emphasize facts and ideas presented in business reports. In addition to clarifying information, charts can help to convey meaning in a more dramatic way. In this lesson you will learn how to create and print a bar chart from the spreadsheet you created in Lesson 4.

Types of Charts

There are eight common types of charts. These charts are listed for you on the format menu on the chart screen. Each chart is unique. The variety of types offers you several qualities from which to choose to best emphasize your spreadsheet information. Here are the eight types:

■ The *bar chart* illustrates information by displaying vertical or horizontal rectangles that compare data by categories or groups. For instance, you could compare estimated sales figures with actual sales figures.

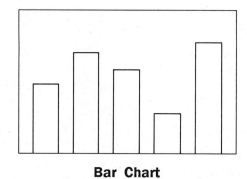

Bar Chart

■ The *stacked bar chart* stacks rectangles on top of one another to create a larger bar. The larger bar presents the combined totals within a category. An example might be to compare the sales figures for three cities.

■ The *100% bar chart* stacks bars on top of one another. This chart emphasizes size based on percentages rather than amounts. It can be used to compare categories as percentages of the whole. An example might be to compare sales for several cities.

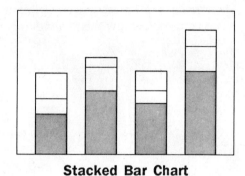

Stacked Bar Chart

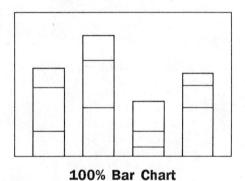

100% Bar Chart

■ The *line chart* is a line of connected dots. It can be used to compare information such as chronological trends.

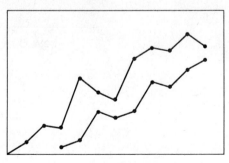

Line Chart

■ The *area line chart* measures and plots each line based on the line below it. It can be used to show the relative importance of different items.

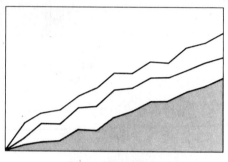

Area Line Chart

■ The *high-low-close chart* emphasizes the range between highs and lows in a category. Stock market figures are usually displayed using this type chart.

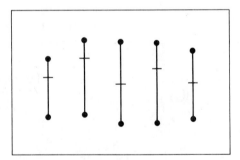

Hi-Low-Close Chart

■ The *pie chart* is a circle divided into pie-shaped sections. It can be used to compare categories to the whole.

■ The *X-Y chart*, also called a scatter chart, plots points along an X-and Y-axis.

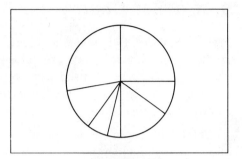

Pie Chart

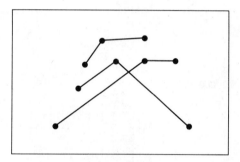

X–Y Chart

Steps to Building a Chart

Study the following steps in creating a simple chart:

1. Plan your chart with pen and paper.

2. Begin with a spreadsheet.

3. Build a chart description.
   a. Specify data and range.
   b. Add headings and labels.

4. Save the chart.

5. Print the chart.

Parts of a Bar Chart

Works provides two ways to create a chart—speed charting (*Works* creates the chart for you) and charting from scratch (you create the chart). Speed charting is used when the ranges you use are adjacent to one another; charting from scratch is used when the ranges are scattered through the spreadsheet. This manual will teach you to speed chart.

Before you begin creating your first chart, study the following example and explanations identifying the various parts of a bar chart.

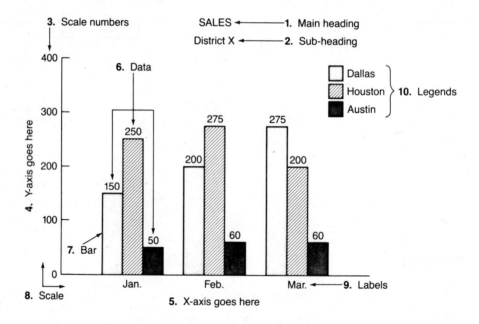

1. The *main heading* may be the heading (text) you used for your spreadsheet; however, you may want to be more descriptive when you create your chart.

2. *Subheadings* help identify the sources of your data. They simply give additional information.

3. *Scale numbers* are added automatically by *Works*.

4. The *Y-axis* runs vertically along the left side of your chart. When you create a chart using speed charting, *Works* will define the Y-series and create legends to label each category.

5. The *X-axis* runs horizontally along the base of the chart. When creating X-Y charts, the purpose is to correlate one type of information with another type of information. In speed charting, *Works* labels the categories along the X-axis.

6. The numerical *data* from within the spreadsheet is portrayed visually by the bars.

7. Each *bar* is usually identified by color, typestyles (fonts), or horizontal grid lines.

8. The *scale numbers* correspond to the straight lines forming the chart's grid.

9. *Labels* name the context for the categories, in this case a time frame.

10. *Legends* identify the categories represented by the patterns or colors in each bar.

Creating a Bar Chart

Now that you have identified the various parts of a bar chart, let's have *Works* create a chart using speed charting from the file named b:SSHEET1.WKS. The chart will compare the expenses for the first quarter of the year.

To create a bar chart, follow these steps:

1. Load the file named b:SSHEET1.WKS if it is not on your screen.

2. Move the cursor to A3.

3. Determine all the cells containing the numbers and the legends and labels that you want to chart.

4. Press F8 and the right- and down-arrow keys to select cells A3 through H9 of the b:SSHEET1.WKS file.

5. From the chart menu, choose the New command (ALT, C, N). The chart screen appears with its menus.

6. From the format menu on the chart screen, choose the bar chart. (ALT, T, B). The chart is created but will not appear on your screen.

7. Press ESC to cancel the highlighting.

Works will automatically add the numbered scale on the Y-axis, the labels on the X-axis, and a legend at the bottom.

Viewing Your Chart

TIP: Make certain you have renamed your screen driver file before viewing your chart. Instructions for renaming are in the Preface.

Now that the chart is created you must use the View command from the chart menu to actually see it.

To view a chart, follow these steps:

1 From the chart menu, choose the View command (ALT, C, V). The chart will appear on your screen.

2 Press ESC to return to the chart screen.

> NOTE: To move to and from the chart and the spreadsheet screens use the following commands:
>
> Chart screen to spreadsheet screen: ALT, C, X
> Spreadsheet or chart screen to chart: ALT, C, V

Adding a Main Heading to the Bar Chart

The next step is to make your bar chart more understandable by adding a main heading. *Works* centers the titles and labels.

To add a main heading, follow these steps:

1 Make certain you are in the chart screen and your spreadsheet is highlighted. (F8, select A3 through H9).

2 From the data menu, choose the Titles command (ALT, D, T). The titles dialog box will appear.

3 Type the first line of the chart title in the chart title text box. Type 1987 EXPENSES

4 Press ALT to highlight the first letters of the commands.

5 Press ALT+S (for subtitle). The cursor moves to subtitle.

6 Type the second line of the chart title in the subtitle text box. Type John Hill

7 Press ALT+X (for X-axis). The cursor moves to the X- axis.

8 Type the X-axis title in the X-axis text box. Type Expenses

9 Press ALT+Y (for Y-axis). The cursor moves to the Y- axis.

10 Type the Y-axis title in the Y-axis text box. Type Cost

11 Type the right Y-axis title in the right Y-axis text box if your chart has a right Y-axis. This example has no right Y- axis.

12 Press ENTER.

13 View your chart again (ALT, C, V).

14 Press ESC to return to the chart screen.

Printing a Chart

One of the most exciting parts of building a chart is seeing it in print. *Works* prints bar charts sideways on a sheet of paper.

To print a chart, follow these steps:

1 From the print menu, choose the Print command (ALT, P, P).

2 The number of copies to be printed in the number of copies text box is set at default one. Press ENTER for one copy. Your chart will print one copy.

3 Press F10 to exit the chart screen.

4 Save the file again (ALT, F, S). *Works* will overwrite the old file and save the chart with it. *Works* considers the chart as part of your spreadsheet. You must always save the file again because *Works* will not allow you to save the chart separately. You may create up to eight charts per spreadsheet.

Your copy should look like the chart on the next page.

Deleting a Chart

You might create a chart but then decide it will not display your information in the best way. For instance, if you created a pie chart and found the

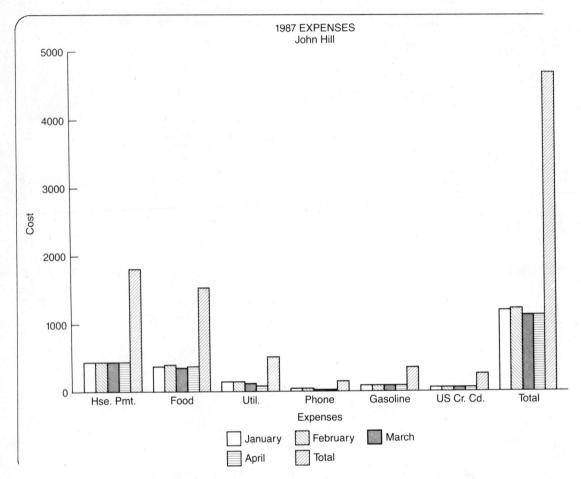

labels were too long and overlapped one another, you would want to delete it and select another kind of chart.

To delete a chart, follow these steps:

1 From the chart menu, choose the chart command (ALT, C, C). The chart dialog box will appear and the last chart you created will be highlighted.

2 Press ALT to highlight the commands available.

3 Highlight the chart to be deleted, in this case chart 1.

4 Press ALT+D (for Delete). The system will prompt you "OK to delete Chart?"

5 Press ENTER to delete the chart.

▬▬▬▬Exiting the Chart Screen

When you finish creating and editing your chart, you can return to the spreadsheet screen.

To leave the chart screen, you can either press F10 or, from the chart menu, choose the Exit Chart command (ALT, C, X).

▬▬▬▬▬Summary▬▬▬▬▬

To Create a Bar Chart:

1. Load the spreadsheet from which you want to create the chart.

2. Determine all the cells containing the numbers and the legends and labels that you want to chart.

3. Press F8 and the right- and down-arrow keys to select the desired cells.

4. From the chart menu, choose the New command (ALT, C, N). The chart screen appears with its menus.

5. From the format menu on the chart screen, choose the bar chart (ALT, T, B). The chart is created but will not appear on your screen.

6. Press ESC to cancel the highlighting.

To View a Chart:

1. From the chart menu, choose the View command (ALT, C, V). The chart will appear on your screen.

2. Press ESC to return to the chart screen.

To Add a Main Heading:

1. Make certain you are in the chart screen and your spreadsheet is highlighted.

2. From the data menu, choose the Titles command (ALT, D, T). The titles dialog box will appear.

3. Type the first line of the chart title in the chart title text box.

4. Press ALT to highlight the first letters of the commands.

5. Press ALT+S (for subtitle). The cursor moves to subtitle.

6. Type the second line of the chart title in the subtitle text box.

7. Press ALT+X (for X-axis). The cursor moves to the X- axis.

8. Type the X-axis title in the X-axis text box.

9. Press ALT+Y (For Y-axis). The cursor moves to the Y- axis.

10. Type the Y-axis title in the Y-axis text box.

11. Type the right Y-axis title in the Right Y-axis text box, if your chart has a right Y-axis. The example in this lesson has no right Y-axis.

12. Press ENTER.

13. View your chart using (ALT, C, V).

14. Press ESC to return to the chart screen.

To Print a Chart:

1. From the print menu, choose the Print command (ALT, P, P).

2. The number of copies to be printed in the number of copies text box is set at one. Press ENTER if you want one copy.

3. Press ENTER. Your chart will print.

To Delete a Chart:

1. From the chart menu, choose the Chart command (ALT, C, C). The chart dialog box will appear, and the last chart you created will be highlighted.

2. Press ALT to highlight the commands available.

3. Highlight the chart to be deleted.

4. Press ALT+D (for delete). The system will prompt you "OK to delete Chart?"

5. Press ENTER to delete the chart.

To Exit the Chart Screen: Press F10 or

From the chart menu, choose the Exit Chart command (ALT, C, X).

6

Database

Without *Works* or some other database program, you might keep records of names and addresses, inventory of equipment, and payroll or other employee information in a card file or reference book of some type. That information can be made more accessible to you by using *Works* to create a database.

What is a database? A database is a tool used for storing and organizing information. Here are some common databases:

Personnel files	Phone lists
Supplier lists	Parts lists
Customer/client list	Name and Address lists

Database commands make it easy for you to search through long, detailed lists for specific information and to add to, delete, extract, or print that information easily.

Since you have used the word processor, the spreadsheet, and charting, the next two lessons will assume you are able to use the basic commands. A reference to commands is given to help you; but refer back to previous lesson summaries should you need assistance.

Terminology Used in Creating a Database

Before you begin working with a database, study the following terms:

- A *field* is a single piece of information such as a name, title, or address. Fields are identified by names or numbers.

- A *record* is several pieces of information put together, such as all the information about one employee—name, address, telephone number, number of tax exemptions, job title, wage per hour, and so forth. Each piece of information is a field.

- A *database* is all individual records put together.

- Like the spreadsheet and charts, it is best to plan your database using pen and paper before starting. Ask yourself the following questions:

  What is the purpose of the database?
  What will be included?
  How can it be organized?
  What categories of information are needed?

- Answering these questions will help you organize and plan your thoughts so that you can set up the database the way you want it the first time.

The Database Screens

Works uses three screens to create databases:

- *The design screen* is used to design your categories of information. The menu bar has three menus that will enable you to create a form. This screen appears first when you enter the database tool. When a form is designed, each entry such as name, address, city, and so on, automatically becomes the fields (column headings) on the form and list screens. Here is a completed design screen:

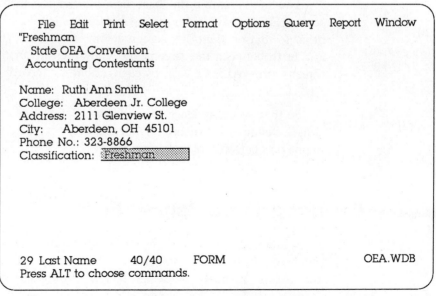

```
 Edit   Format   Window
 State OEA Convention
 Accounting Contestants

Name:
College: _____
Address: _____
City:
Phone No.: _____
Classification: _____




Pg 1                          Design                        OEA.WDB
Type field names. Press ALT to choose commands or F10 to exit Form Design.
```

Figure 6-1 Design Screen

■ *The form screen* is used to add information onto each form. You can work with one record at a time, just as you would if you were working with a card file. Here is a completed form screen:

```
    File   Edit   Print   Select   Format   Options   Query   Report   Window
"Freshman
   State OEA Convention
 Accounting Contestants

Name:  Ruth Ann Smith
College:  Aberdeen Jr. College
Address: 2111 Glenview St.
City:    Aberdeen, OH 45101
Phone No.: 323-8866
Classification:  Freshman




29 Last Name      40/40     FORM                        OEA.WDB
Press ALT to choose commands.
```

Figure 6-2 Form Screen

■ The list screen is used to prepare databases in a listing format. Here is a completed list screen:

File	Edit	Print	Select	Format	Options	Query	Report	Window			

```
"Beamon
              Name              College            Address           City           Phone No.   Classification
   1    Hillary Moore    Elmhearst Jr. College   2323 Bradbury Drive   Cincinnati, OH 45207   457-9090   Freshman
   2    John Morrison    Wright Junior College   112 N.W. 108th        Reily, OH 45056        458-9644   Freshman
   3    Jennifer Munez   Salazar Com. College    6733 Beach Street     Dayton, OH 45444       388-0895   Freshman
   4    Ruth Ann Smith   Aberdeen Jr. College    2111 Glenview         Aberdeen, OH 45101     323-8866   Freshman
   5    Juanita Ruiz     Carrera Jr. College     5656 College Drive    Cincinnati, OH 45248   485-2727   Freshman
   6
   7
   8
   9
  10
  11
  12
  13
  14
  15
  16
  17
  18
  19
  20
   1  Name        5/5        LIST                                                              OEA.WDB
Press ALT to choose commands.
```

Figure 6-3 List Screen

You may create a database using either the form screen or the list screen. Either way, *Works* automatically creates the same database in the other format on the other screen at the same time. You can switch back and forth between the screens and view the information as a whole (list screen—press ALT, O, V) or by each individual record (form screen—press ALT, O, V).

So that you may learn to work with databases, we will begin with a simple customer list (listing name, address, city, state, ZIP, area code, and phone number) to explain the procedures.

Designing the Database Form

Your database form is designed from the design screen. You will enter the database tool from the new menu just as you entered the word processor and the spreadsheet. The design screen will appear first.

Works assumes you want to create the form first. Use the design screen to create and name the fields that will make up your database.

To design a form, follow these steps:

1. From the design screen, space six times to center the title; type Customer List.

2. Press the down-arrow key two times to leave a blank line after the heading.

3. Type Name: (Be sure to type the colon after name and do not type quotation marks before the entry.) Press ENTER. A blank line will appear to the right of the entry. The blank line is ten characters long.

4. Because names take up quite a bit of space, widen the blank line to 24 (ALT, T, W, 24, ENTER). You will see the number 16 appear in the Width dialog box. Name, colon, and a space is equal to six characters, then ten characters for the blank line adds to 16. Each Width dialog box number will vary depending on the entry you typed.

5. Press the down arrow once.

6. Type Address: and press ENTER

7. Because addresses also require quite a lot of space, widen that column to 24 also (ALT, T, W, 24, ENTER).

8. Press the down arrow once.

9. Type the remaining labels, pressing the down-arrow once after each entry :

> City: (widen to 24 characters)
> State:
> ZIP:
> Area Code:
> Telephone No.:

Move your cursor to Name with the up arrow. Your screen should look like Figure 6.4.

Entering Data from the Form Screen

You have just created the categories (fields) you will be working with in this lesson. Data may be entered record by record from the form screen or from the list screen much like data in a spreadsheet. Entering the data in

```
┌─────────────────────────────────────────────────────────────────────┐
│                                                                       │
│        Edit    Format    Window                                       │
│      Name:                                                            │
│              Customer List                                            │
│                                                                       │
│      Name: _____                         │
│      Address: _____                        │
│      City: _____                        │
│      State: _____                              │
│      ZIP: _____                                    │
│      Area Code: _____                     │
│      Telephone No.: _____                  │
│                                                                       │
│                                                                       │
│                                                                       │
│      Pg 1                      DESIGN                    DATA1.WDB     │
│      Type field names. Press ALT to choose commands or F10 to exit Form Design. │
│                                                                       │
└─────────────────────────────────────────────────────────────────────┘
```

Figure 6-4

one screen also enters it in the other. Let's learn to enter data from the form screen.

To enter data from the form screen, follow these steps:

1. After designing the form, press F10 to go to the form screen.

2. Move your cell cursor to Name.

3. Type Jill L. Jordan (the name will appear on the formula bar).

4. Press the down-arrow once.

5. Type 120 Hill St.

6. Press the down-arrow once.

7. Type Dallas

8. Press the down arrow once.

9. Type the rest of the information for Jill Jordan. When you enter the last information, press the down arrow and the system will take you to the form for the next name. When your cursor is on the Phone No. your screen should look like this for Jill Jordan:

```
     File   Edit   Print   Select   Format   Options   Query   Report   Window
  *681-2234
            Customer List

  Name:   Jill L. Jordan
  Address:  120 Hill Street
  City:    Dallas
  State:   TX
  ZIP:       75222
  Area Code      214
  Telephone No.      681-2234




  1   Telephone No.   1/1    FORM                              DATA1.WDB
  Press ALT to choose commands or CTRL+PGDN/PGUP for next/previous record.
```

Figure 6-5

[10] Enter all the data for the rest of your customer list. If a series of numbers begin with zero (0), as in the ZIP code for Boston, precede the zero with a quotation mark so the zero will print.

Jill L. Jordan	120 Hill Street	Dallas	TX	75222	214	681-2234
James K. Marshall	9036 Audelia St.	Dallas	TX	75223	214	328-1122
R.M. Woodward	1015 S. Main St.	Ft. Worth	TX	76110	817	294-8192
Mark Maloney	2535 May Ct.	Ft. Worth	TX	76112	817	531-4848
Marie Aloe	2887 George St.	Dallas	TX	75244	214	239-0045
Julie Gentry	1424 Yucca St.	Midlothian	TX	76065	214	775-3210
Paul Porter	3939 Fortune	San Jose	CA	95131	408	942-4466
David R. Moore	1213 Graham St.	Boston	MA	O2108	617	725-4589
Betty Jones	1212 Burr Oak	Arlington	TX	76012	817	277-8832
Bill Hargrove	221 Bordon Rd.	San Antonio	TX	78280	512	497-7645

Figure 6-6

[11] Proofread your data.

12 Save the file. Name it b:DATA1.WDB (ALT, F, A).

TIP: Use CTRL-PGUP and CTRL-PGDN to quickly move from one record to another when using the form screen.

Viewing the Database from the List Screen

While you were entering the data record by record from the form screen, *Works* was also recording the data in the form of a list. Let's view the list and learn how to format it to make it easier to read.

To view and format the database from the list screen, follow these steps:

1 Press ALT, O (for options), V (for View List) to view the database from the list screen.

2 Notice that the name and address columns need to be widened. Move your cursor to the name column and widen it to 24 spaces (ALT, T, W, 24, ENTER).

3 Move the cursor to the address column with the right arrow and widen that column to 24 spaces also (ALT, T, W, 24, ENTER).

4 Move the cursor to the city column with the right arrow and widen that column to 12 spaces (ALT, T, W, 12, ENTER).

5 Move the cursor to the state column and center the states (ALT, T, S, ALT, C, ENTER).

6 Center the ZIP Code column (ALT, T, S, ALT, C, ENTER).

7 Center the area code column (ALT, T, S, ALT, C, ENTER).

8 Save the file with its changes (ALT, F, S).

9 Print one copy of the file (ALT, P, ENTER, ENTER).

10 Leave the file on your screen.

Your copy should look like this (your copy will print on two pages):

Jill L. Jordan	120 Hill Street	Dallas	TX	75222	214	681-2234
James K. Marshall	9036 Audelia St.	Dallas	TX	75223	214	328-1122
R.M. Woodward	1015 S. Main St.	Ft. Worth	TX	76110	817	294-8192
Mark Maloney	2535 May Ct.	Ft. Worth	TX	76112	817	531-4848
Marie Aloe	2887 George St.	Dallas	TX	75244	214	239-0045
Julie Gentry	1424 Yucca St.	Midlothian	TX	76065	214	775-3210
Paul Porter	3939 Fortune	San Jose	CA	95131	408	942-4466
David R. Moore	1213 Graham St.	Boston	MA	02108	617	725-4589
Betty Jones	1212 Burr Oak	Arlington	TX	76012	817	277-8832
Bill Hargrove	221 Bordon Rd.	San Antonio	TX	78280	512	497-7645

Figure 6-7

Querying (Searching or Questioning) the Database

You can query the database to locate specific data such as all the customers who live in Dallas. *Works* will search through the data, extract it, and move it to the query screen. You can then print a copy. Let's learn how to extract data by querying the database for all customers from Dallas.

To query, follow these steps:

1 Move to the form screen (ALT, O, V from the list screen or F10 from the design screen).

2 Choose the query menu, then choose Define (ALT, Q, D).

3 Move your cursor to City.

4 Type Dallas (you are defining the query).

5 Press ENTER.

6 Press F10.

7 Go to the list screen (ALT, O, V). There will be a list of the names of the customers from Dallas.

8   Print one copy of the customers (ALT, P, ENTER, ENTER).

9   Save and name the file b:QUERY. Press ENTER.

10   Clear the screen (ALT, F, C).

Entering Data from the List Screen

Often it is easier to make lists directly on the list screen rather than developing a record for each one first. Remember, *Works* will develop a separate record automatically. Using the following example, create a database from the list screen.

Last Name	First Name	Middle Initial
Johnson	David	L.
Ounnarath	Seng	
Miller	James	Frances
Seymour	Pat	A.
Bates	Terri	K.
Alexander	Harold	Michael
Boyd	Cody	E.
Miller	Allen	B.
McAvoy	Myrna	Louise
Iverson	Dee Ann	L.
Forbus	Mike	Allen
Alexander	Johnny	B.
Miller	Charles	R.

To enter data from the list screen, follow these steps:

1   Enter the database tool and move to the list screen (F10, ALT, O, V).

2   Move the cursor to any cell in the field you want. Move to line 1 at the left.

3   From the edit menu, choose the Name command (ALT, E, N).

4   Type the first field name in the name text box. Type Last Name.

5   Press ENTER.

6   Widen the cell to 20 spaces (ALT, T, W, 20, ENTER).

7   Press the right arrow once.

8   From the edit menu, choose the Name command (ALT, E, N) and type the second field name in the name text box. Type First Name. Press ENTER.

9   Widen the cell to 20 spaces (ALT, T, W, 20, ENTER).

10   Press the right arrow once.

11   From the edit menu, choose the Name command (ALT, E, N) and type the third field name in the name text box. Type Middle Initial. Press ENTER.

12   Widen the cell to 20 spaces (ALT, T, W, 20, ENTER).

13   Move the cursor to line 1 at the left and enter the names in the example into your database. When you finish, leave the file on your screen.

Sorting

Works can sort your database in either ascending (A–Z) or descending (Z–A) order. The default is ascending order. *Works* will alphabetize, ignoring upper-and lower-case. You identify the field names you want sorted—field 1, field 2, field 3. *Works* will sort in that order. An example would be the database names you entered, field 1—last name, field 2—first name, field 3—middle initial.

To sort in ascending order, follow these steps:

1   From the query menu, choose the Sort command (ALT, Q, S). The Sort dialog box will appear.

2   *Works* assumes you will sort beginning with the first field; therefore, its name already appears on the first field line. The system will save your field names once they are entered so you can use them to sort later.

3   Press ALT. The first letters are highlighted.

4   Press ALT+2 and type the name of the second field. Type First Name

5   Press ALT+3 and type the name of the third field. Type Middle Initial

6   Press ENTER to sort.

7   Print one copy of your file (ALT, P, ENTER, ENTER).

8   Save the file (ALT, F, A). Name the file b:DATA2.WDB.

9 Clear the screen (ALT, F,C).

Your copy should look like this:

Alexander	Harold	Michael
Alexander	Johnny	B.
Bates	Terri	K.
Boyd	Cody	E.
Forbus	Mike	Allen
Iverson	Dee Ann	L.
Johnson	David	L.
McAvoy	Myrna	Louise
Miller	Allen	B.
Miller	Charles	R.
Miller	James	Frances
Ounnarath	Seng	
Seymour	Pat	A

Many of the commands you learned using the spreadsheet will apply to your database. You can edit cells, copy, move columns or rows, and use many other commands provided on the database menus.

━━━━ Summary ━━━━

To Design a Form:

1. From the Design screen type the title at the desired position.

2. Press the down-arrow key two times to leave a blank line after the heading.

3. Type the first field name.

4. Widen the field if necessary. Press the down-arrow.

5. Type the remaining fields, pressing the down-arrow key once after each entry and widening the fields as necessary.

To Enter Data from the Form Screen:

1. After designing the form, press F10 to go to the form screen.

2. Move your cursor to the first entry.

3. Enter the information.

4. Press the down-arrow once.

5. Enter the remaining information. After each entry, press the down-arrow once.

6. After the last entry, press the down-arrow once to go to the next blank form.

To View and Format the Database From the List Screen:

1. Press ALT, O (for options), V (for view list) to view the database from the list screen.

2. Determine if the columns need to be widened and widen them if necessary.

3. Center any field names that need centering (ALT, T, S, ALT, C, ENTER).

To Query a Database:

1. Move to the form screen (ALT, O, V from the list screen or F10 from the design screen).

2. Choose the query menu; then choose Define (ALT, Q, D).

3. Move the cursor to the field to be queried.

4. Define the query.

5. Press ENTER.

6. Press F10.

7. Go to the list screen (ALT, O, V). The query will be listed.

8. Clear the screen (ALT, F, C).

To Enter Data From the List Screen:

1. Move to the list screen (ALT, O, V).

2. Move the cursor to any cell in the field you want.

3. From the edit menu, choose the Name command (ALT, E, N).

4. Type the first field name in the name text box.

5. Press ENTER.

6. Widen the cell if necessary.

7. Press the right arrow once.

8. From the edit menu, choose the Name command (ALT, E, N) and type the second field name in the name text box.

9. Widen the cell if necessary.

10. Press the right arrow once.

11. From the edit menu, choose the Name command (ALT, E, N) and type the third field name in the name text box.

12. Widen the cell if necessary.

13. Move the cursor to line 1 at the left and enter the data into your database.

To Sort:

1. From the query menu, choose the Sort command (ALT, Q, S). The Sort dialog box will appear.

2. *Works* assumes you will sort beginning with the first field; therefore, its name already appears on the first field line. The system will save your field names once they are entered so you can use them to sort later.

3. Press ALT. The first letters are highlighted. Press ALT and then choose the order.

4. Press ALT+2 and type the name of the second field. Choose the order.

5. Press ALT+3 and type the name of the third field. Choose the order.

6. Press ENTER to sort.

7. Save the file, print as needed, and clear the screen.

7

Communications

Another easy-to-use software package included on your disk is *Works'* communications program. What is communications? Communications lets you share information between two computers via a direct cable or via telephone lines. A modem (short for modulator/demodulator) turns electrical signals from your computer into signals that can be transmitted by phone lines. Modems may be internal (installed in your computer) or external (attached to your computer by a cable).

Communications makes a variety of services available:

Travel information and shopping
News services
Electronic banking
Dating services
Electronic mail
Library searches
Research
Medicine or law
Electronic bulletin boards

Other capabilities of communications systems are
Sending and receiving messages
Sending and receiving data
Setting up a personal dialing directory
Emulating (mimicking) another computer terminal

This lesson assumes you have a modem. You will learn how to open or create a communications file, use the connect command, sign on to an information service, send and receive information, and end your communications session. You will need to check with your instructor for the phone numbers and parameters (system requirements) of the local information service or other computers you will be calling.

▬▬▬Basic Steps in a Communications Session

There are four basic steps in a communications session, no matter how you are sending or receiving information:

1. Open or create a communications file.

2. Connect with the other computer.

3. Communicate with the other computer.

4. Disconnect and close your communications file.

The *host* computer is the other computer to which you are connected.

▬▬▬Entering the Communications Tool

You enter the communications tool the same way you entered the other three tools.

To enter the communications tool, follow these steps:

From the new menu, choose the communications tool (ALT, C, ENTER). The communications screen will appear.

The Communications Screen

The communications screen is similar to the ones you have used for the other tools. It is a screen that allows you to see the information sent by the computer to which you are connected. It also stores the settings and phone number necessary to call the other computer.

Here is the communications screen; locate the parts on your screen as each part is discussed.

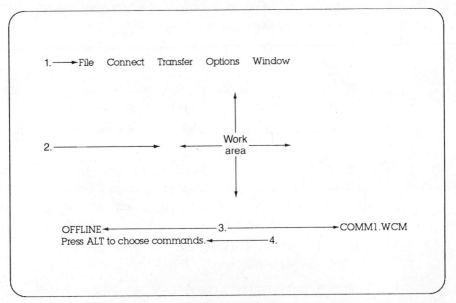

Figure 7-1

1. The *menu bar* runs across the top of the screen. It displays the communications menus, which contain the commands necessary to send and receive information.

2. The *work area* is the blank space where you can type or display information you are sending or receiving.

3. The *status line* helps you keep up with your work. It displays OFFLINE when you are not connected and a clock that will run when you are connected to another computer. It also identifies the name of the current file you are using.

4. The *message line* provides hints and descriptions of the commands in the menu bar.

▬▬▬▬▬ Creating a Communications File

The first step in starting a communications session is to create and save a communications file for the computer you are calling. Once this file is saved, you can use it over and over when you call that particular computer.

In the course of using the communications tool, you will develop several files—one for each computer you call. You need to contact the person or service you are calling and obtain certain information about their computer to set up a communications file. You need to know the following (*Works'* default settings are in parentheses):

■ *Baud Rate*—how many characters per second are sent or received? A common baud rate is 1200. (1200)

■ *Databits*—the number of electrical signals required to define a character. A common number of databits is 8. (8)

■ *Stopbits*—the number of electrical signals that mark the end of a character. A common number of stopbits is 1. (1)

■ *Handshake* (X-on/X-off)—allows two computers to send hardware or software back and forth, exchange Pause and Continue signals, or indicate to each other when they are ready to send or receive information. Both computers must support the same type of handshaking. (Xon/Xoff)

■ *Parity*—the kind of error-checking procedure used. A common setting is MASK. (MASK)

■ *Port*—represents the name of a communications port, followed by a colon. A common port used with modems is COM1:. (COM1)

If you are setting up a communications file for an information service, the service will provide the above information. The default settings in this text are commonly used by most information services.

Most information services provide material such as the day's news headlines, stock market information, the weather, health-related information, the latest developments in medicine, and many other types of information. A fee is charged monthly or quarterly. Once you have subscribed to the service, a password and an I.D. number, as well as all the information about their computer are given to you to enable you to make a connection. Ask your instructor for your local information service's name, phone number, and any other setup information you need to create a communications file.

To create a communications file, follow these steps:

1. Choose the Terminal command from the options menu to make your computer agree with the computer you are calling (ALT, O, T). The terminal dialog box will appear. Ask your instructor if you should make any changes in these settings. The settings are:

   Terminal type: VT52 or ANSI. (Default is VT52.)

   Local Echo: Causes the host computer (the one you are calling) not to echo back (print on your screen) what is sent or received. (Default is nothing selected.)

   Wraparound: Causes incoming lines of type to wraparound at the right screen margin. (Default is X.)

   Fullscreen: Allows you to take advantage of the fullscreen for viewing—the menu bars, status and prompt lines disappear. (Default is nothing selected.)

   Add to Incoming Lines: Use this setting if you need to add carriage returns (CR) or line feed (LF) to each line of text the host computer sends you. (Default is nothing.) Choose line feed (ALT, ALT +L). An X will appear in the parentheses.

   Key Pad Alternate: Puts your key pad into the application mode when NUM LOCK is on. (Default is nothing selected.)

   Cursor Alternate: Puts your cursor keys into application mode when NUM LOCK is off. (Default is nothing selected.)

   Press ENTER when finished or to accept the default or make changes directed by your instructor.

2. Make any needed changes in the communications defaults (ALT, O, C). The communications dialog box appears showing all defaults. Check with your instructor about the changes to be made. Press ENTER when you are finished or to accept the default.

3. Make any needed changes in the phone defaults (ALT, O, P). The phone dialog box appears showing all defaults. Type the phone number of the computer you are calling. If you normally dial 9 for an outside line, enter 9 and a comma before you enter the phone number. (You may enter a hyphen in the phone number to separate the digits.)

4. *Works* uses the Hayes command set (sometimes called the AT commands) to control your modem. This means *Works* will operate best using Hayes-compatible modems that can respond to these commands. The commands

are entered at the modem setup line (ALT+M). Ask your instructor if you should enter any Hayes commands. If your modem is Hayes compatible, *Works* will enter the commands for you. Some common AT commands are

ATL1X3 tells the computer to dial a number.

AT instructs the computer to dial.

L1 lowers the speaker volume.

X3 displays BUSY for a busy signal.

5 Press ENTER.

6 Save the file. Use your information service name as the name of the file so it can easily be identified (ALT, F, A, FILENAME, ENTER.) Be sure to precede your file name with b:

NOTE: If you have already created a communications file, choose Open from the file menu to open an existing file (ALT, F, O, FILENAME, ENTER).

TIP: If your settings are not correct and your computer will not respond, you are locked in an error mode and should press Ctrl-ALT- Del.

Making a Connection with an Information Service

The Connect command is used to contact another computer. *Works* will use the communications file you created or opened, dial the number you entered, and make a connection with the other computer when it answers the phone via your modem. In the upper left corner of your screen, you will see when the connection is made. All connections are made this way.

To make a connection, follow these steps:

1 Open the communications file for the information service you are calling, if it is not already open.

2 From the connect menu, choose the Connect command (ALT, C, C).

3 Wait for feedback from the modem. You will hear the number dialed, a ring, a high pitch tone, then static. Your screen might look something like Figure 7-2. In the upper corner, ATDT (phone number) tells the modem to dial this number. A timer will replace the message OFFLINE on the status line. When the host computer answers, you will see the word *Connect* on your screen.

```
        File    Connect   Transfer   Options   Window
     ATDT638-4150
     CONNECT

     Enter ID #: 22541091




     .00:00:56                                    INFOTEXT.WCM
     Press ALT to choose commands.
```

Figure 7-2

4 Respond to the logon prompts of the service you are calling, giving your password and I.D. number. Your password may not print on the screen as you enter it. It you wait too long to respond, the screen will disconnect and you will see the statement NO CARRIER appear. You will then have to end your communication session or press ALT, C, D to dial again. Your communications service may have a logoff procedure. Ask your instructor for the procedure you are to use. The words NO CARRIER should appear on your screen when you have properly logged off the service.

Ending Your Communications Session

You must disconnect from the computer transmission, just as you would hang up a telephone from a phone conversation.

To end your communications session, follow these steps:

1 Choose the connect command from the connect menu again (ALT, C, C). A dialog box will appear asking "OK to disconnect?"

2 Press ENTER for OK. Your status line will show the word OFFLINE when the communication is broken.

3 | Choose close from the file menu (ALT, F, C) to close the communications file. You will be asked if you want to save changes to the file each time you use a file over and over. Simply press ENTER each time.

▬▬▬ Answering a Call

When your computer is being called to receive information, you must set your computer to receive the information.

To answer a call, follow these steps:

1 | Create a communications file containing the settings for compatibility with the computer calling you. See "Creating a Communications File" earlier in this lesson.

2 | Choose phone from the options menu (ALT, O, P). The phone dialog box appears.

3 | Press ALT+A for automatic answer. Make certain there is no information in the phone number or modem setup lines if your modem is Hayes Compatible.

4 | Press ENTER.

5 | Choose the connect command from the connect menu (ALT, C, C).

Your screen should look something like this.

```
    File   Connect   Transfer   Options   Window
ATSO=1
OK




.00:00:20                    ANSW              MICROSFT.WCM
Press ALT to choose commands.
```

Figure 7-3

Wait for a message or file to appear on your screen. Respond to any messages after you see the word OVER or OK.

6 Choose the connect command from the connect menu to disconnect (ALT, C, C, ENTER) when you are finished.

Sending and Receiving Information

After you have made a connection with another computer, you can send and receive information using the transfer menu in one of three ways: by typing and displaying text, by downloading files, and by uploading files.

Typing and Displaying Text (Conversational Style)

Whatever you type is sent out via your modem or direct cable and appears on the host computer's display. This is known as conversational style. You and the operator of the host computer can type messages back and forth to one another. Ask your instructor how this exercise is to be completed. You will need a host computer set for "Answering a Call" (see the previous section). Thus you will need to agree on a time at which both you and the other operator can be at your computers to set up the equipment and respond back and forth by typing messages on your screens.

To send text conversational style (transfer text as you type it), follow these steps:

1 Open the communications file for the host computer. Be sure to turn automatic answer off and enter a phone number for the computer you are calling.

2 Connect to the host computer (ALT, C, C). The Hayes command ATDT followed by the host computer's phone number and the word CONNECT will appear on your screen. That is when you may begin typing.

3 Type your message. Type: Working with computers is a challenge. Do you agree? (Press ENTER once)

OVER (Press ENTER)

Wait for a response.

4 After you are finished communicating, end your session (ALT, C, C, EN-TER).

5 Clear your screen (ALT, F, C).

NOTE: When typing your messages, if your words do not wrap around to the next line, but are stacking at the right margin, you can press ALT, O, T to choose the terminal command and select wraparound (ALT, ALT+W). If the cursor returns to the left margin and types over the same line, choose LF (line-feed) from the terminal command and the cursor will advance a line. (ALT, O, T, ALT, ALT+L, ENTER).

Downloading (Receiving) Files

When someone is sending you a file or program (called downloading), you must set your machine to answer just as you did when receiving conversational style text. A communications file is created, a connection is made, and you must choose either the *Capture Text* command or the *Receive Protocol* command depending on the type of file you will be receiving. The *Capture text* command saves the information that appears on your screen to a file so that later you can print, edit, or include it in another file. The *Recieve Protocol* command allows you to transfer a file from another computer to a file on your disk. Let's set our machine to receive a formatted file such as a spreadsheet we have created in an earlier chapter.

To receive a file using the receive protocol command, follow these steps:

1 Open a communications file and make a connection with your host computer (ALT, C, C).

2 Choose the transfer menu then the Receive Protocol command (ALT, T, R).

3 A Save As dialog box appears asking you to enter a name for the file. Type the name b:SS1.WKS. Make certain you enter the extension or the file will not be saved. Your host computer should proceed to the next exercise and send you the file named b:SSHEET1.WKS created in an earlier chapter. The default for the file type is binary. Since the file named b:SHEET1.WKS is a formatted file you do not have to change the default setting.

4 Press ENTER. During the transfer a status box displays telling you the status of the transfer, how many bytes have been received, and how many

errors and retries have occurred. When the entire file has been transferred, the status line in the status box changes to "transfer successful."
You may abort the transfer any time by pressing ESC. Press ENTER and
choose OK to continue your communications session.

5 Check your file directory to see if the filename is there (ALT, F, O). Open
and close the file.

6 Advise the host computer if the file transfer was successful or not by typing a message.

7 End your communications session (ALT, C, C, ENTER) and close the file
(ALT, F, C).

Uploading (Sending) Files

To send a file from your computer (called uploading) to another computer's
disk, you must open the host computer's file, and make a connection just as
you have done previously. There are two commands used to upload files.
The *Send Text* command is like typing text, only faster. You can type the
text using the word processor and send it line by line to another computer.
The *Send Protocol* command is used to transfer a file from your disk to another computer's disk. Let's send the spreadsheet created in an earlier
chapter named b:SSHEET1.WKS.

To send a file using the Send Protocol command, follow these steps:

1 Open the host computer's communications file and make a connection
(ALT, C, C) and tell the computer to get ready to receive by typing a message.

2 Choose the Send Protocol command from the transfer menu (ALT, T, S).

3 A Send Protocol dialog box will appear asking you to type the name of the
file to be sent. Type the file name b:SSHEET1.WKS and press ENTER.

4 During the transfer a status box displays telling you the status of the
transfer, how many bytes have been sent, how many errors and retries
have occurred. The transfer status line in the dialog box will alternate between send and waiting as the file is sent. When the complete file is sent,
the transfer status line will indicate "transfer successful." If more than ten
tries occur, *Works* cancels the transfer. You may press ESC to abort the
transfer at any time.

⑤ Press ENTER to continue your communications session. Wait for a message telling you if the transfer was received successfully.

⑥ End your communications session by disconnecting (ALT, C, C, ENTER) and closing the file (ALT, F, C).

Again, before beginning, check with your instructor about procedures for completing this exercise.

▬▬▬▬▬▬Summary▬▬▬▬▬▬

To Create a Communications File:

1. Make any needed changes in the Terminal default from the options menu (ALT, O, T) and press ENTER.

2. Make any needed changes in the communications defaults from the options menu (ALT, O, C) and press ENTER.

3. Enter the phone number using the Phone command from the options menu (ALT, O, P).

4. Press ENTER.

5. Save the file (ALT, F, A).

To Make a Connection:

1. Open the communications file for the host computer you are calling if it is not already open.

2. From the connect menu, choose the Connect command (ALT, C, C).

3. Wait for feedback from the modem. The timer should begin when you are connected.

4. Respond to the logon prompts if you are calling an information service or wait for a message if you are answering a call.

To End Your Communications Session:

1. Choose the connect command from the connect menu again (ALT, C, C). A dialog box will appear asking "OK to disconnect?"

2. Press ENTER for OK. Your status line will show the word OFFLINE when the communication is broken.

3. Choose close from the file menu (ALT, F, C) to close the communications file.

To Answer a Call:

1. Create a communications file containing the settings for compatibility with the computer calling you.

2. Choose phone from the options menu (ALT, O, P). The phone dialog box appears.

3. Press ALT+A for automatic answer. Make certain the phone number and modem setup lines are blank if your modem is Hayes compatible.

4. Press ENTER.

5. Choose the connect command from the connect menu (ALT, C, C). Wait for a message or file to appear on your screen. Respond to any messages after you see the word OVER or OK.

6. Choose the connect command from the connect menu to disconnect (ALT, C, C) when you are finished.

To Send Text Conversational Style:

1. Open the communications file for the host computer.

2. Connect to the host's computer (ALT, C, C).

3. Type your message. When you type all the way across the screen *Works* will wordwrap. Wait for a response.

4. After you are finished communicating, end your communications session (ALT, C, C, ENTER).

5. Clear your screen (ALT, F, C).

To Download (Receive) a File Using the Receive Protocol Command:

1. Open a communications file and make a connection with your host computer (ALT, C, C).

2. Choose the Transfer menu then the Receive Protocol command (ALT, T, R).

3. A Save As dialog box appears asking you to enter a name for the file. Make certain you enter the extension or the file will not be saved. Precede the filename with b:

4. Press ENTER. During the transfer a status box displays telling you the status of the transfer, how many bytes have been transmitted, and how many errors and retries have occurred. When the entire file has been transferred, the status line in the status box changes to "transfer successful." You may abort the transfer any time by pressing ESC. Press ENTER and choose OK to continue your communications session.

5. Check your file directory to see if the filename is there (ALT, F, 0). Open and close the file.

6. Advise the host computer if the file transfer was successful or not.

7. End your communications session (ALT, C, C, ENTER) and close the file (ALT, F, C).

To Upload (Send) a File Using the Send Protocol Command:

1. Open the host computer's communications file and make a connection (ALT, C, C) and tell the computer to get ready to receive by typing a message.

2. Choose the Send Protocol command from the transfer menu (ALT, T, S).

3. A Send Protocol dialog box will appear asking you to type the name of the file to be sent. Type the name of the file. During the transfer a status box displays telling you the status of the transfer, how many bytes have been sent, how many errors and retries have occurred. The transfer status line in the dialog box will alternate between send and waiting as the file is sent. When the complete file is sent, the transfer status line will indicate "transfer successful." If more than ten tries occur, *Works* cancels the transfer.

4. Press ENTER to continue your communications session. Wait for a message telling you if the transfer was received successfully.

5. End your communications session by disconnecting (ALT, C, C, ENTER) and closing the file (ALT, F, C).

Appendix A

Microsoft *Works* Summary of Commands

General Commands

Enter *Works*	*Works*
Select Command	ALT,Letter,Letter
Cancel Command	ESC
Exit *Works*	ALT,F,X
Print a File	ALT,P,ENTER,ENTER
Print Without Page Numbers	ALT,P,L,ALT,ALT+F,BACKSPACE, ENTER,ALT,P,ENTER,ENTER
Close a File	ALT,F,C
Open a File	ALT,F,O,FILENAME,ENTER
Save a File	ALT,F,A,FILENAME,ENTER

Word Processor Commands

View Menus	ALT,F,Right Arrow
Create a Document	Enter *Works* and Type
Move Cursor	Ctrl-HOME—Beginning of File
	Cursor Right—Right Arrow
	Cursor Left—Left Arrow
	Down a Line—Down Arrow
	Up a Line—Up Arrow
	HOME—Beginning of Line
	END—End of Line
	Ctrl-END—End of File
	Ctrl-Right Arrow—Whole Words Right
	Ctrl-Left Arrow—Whole Words Left
Underline	Position Cursor, F8, Highlight,ESC,ALT,T,U
Delete Characters	Position Cursor, Press DEL Key

| Delete Blocks of Text | Position Cursor at Beginning, F8, Highlight, ESC, ALT, E,D |
| Insert Text | Position Cursor Where Text Is To Go, Type Text |

Spreadsheet Commands

Select	F8,Use Arrow Keys to Highlight
GoTo Command	F5,Reference Location, ENTER
Clear a Cell	ALT,E,E
Align Columns Right	F8,Highlight,ALT,T,S,Move Cursor to Right, ENTER,ESC
Copy	Position Cursor in Cell to be Copied,F8,Highlight Cells To Copy to, ALT,E,R,ESC
Edit a Cell	Position Cursor in Cell,F2, HOME, Delete Entry, Type New, ENTER
Display Formulas	Position Cursor in Formula Cell,ALT,O,F
Insert a Column	Position Cursor, ALT,S,C, ALT,E,I,ESC
Delete a Column	Position Cursor,ALT, S,C,ALT,E,D,ESC
Move a Column	Position Cursor,ALT, S,C,ALT,E,M, Select New Position ALT,S,C, ENTER

Chart Commands

Create A Bar Chart	Open Spreadsheet File,F8 Highlight Cells,ALT,C,N,ALT, T,B,ESC
View a Chart	ALT,C,V,ESC when finished
Exit Chart Screen	ALT,C,X

Database Commands

To Query   Move to Form Screen,ALT,Q,D,
                            Move Cursor to Query Field,
                            Define Query,ENTER, F10,ALT,
                            O,V

To Sort   ALT,Q,S,Identify Each
                            Field,ENTER

Communications Commands

Create a Communications File   ALT,O,T,Make Changes,ENTER
                            ALT,O,C,Make Changes,ENTER
                            ALT,O,P,Enter Information,
                            ENTER,Save the file

Make a Connection   Open Communications File,
                            ALT,C,C,Respond to
                            Requested Information

Disconnect   ALT,C,C,ENTER

Answer a Call   Open Communications File,
                            ALT,O,P,ALT+A,ENTER,
                            ALT,C,C

Send Text Conversational
  Style   Open Communications File,
                            Connect ALT,C,C,Type Messages
                            Disconnect ALT,C,C,ENTER

Download (Receive) a File
  Using Receive Protocol   Open Communications File,
                            Connect ALT,C,C,ALT,T,R,
                            Type name of file,ENTER,
                            Advise received,ALT,C,C,
                            ENTER,ALT,F,C

Upload (Send) a File Using
  Send Protocol   Open Communications File,
                            Connect ALT,C,C,ALT,T,S,
                            Type name of file,ENTER,
                            ALT,C,C,ALT,F,C

Appendix B

▰▰▰▰ Hard (Fixed) Disk System

If you have a hard disk system, make certain you review the operating manual that came with the system. You should have the DOS (disk operating system) already loaded onto your hard disk. Here are some generic instructions that are basic to most hard disk systems:

To Create a Works Directory:

1. Load DOS. The C> should show on your screen.

2. Enter md\works (md means make directory. Be sure to use the backslash and not the forward slash mark).

3. Press Return. You have just created a space on your hard disk for *Works Educational Version*.

To Load Works onto Your Hard Disk:

1. Change the *Works* sub-directory (cd\works).

2. Insert the *Works Educational Version* program disk in Drive A.

3. Type Copy a:*.* and RETURN.

4. Remove the *Works Educational Version* disk when copying is complete.

Booting Works:

1. Turn on your computer to the C:\>prompt.

2. Enter: cd\works and RETURN.

3. Enter: Works and RETURN. The Works title screen will appear.

Appendix C

Formatting a Disk

If you need to format a disk to use as a data disk to save your spread-sheets, graphs, etc. Follow these steps:

To Format a Disk (Single-Disk-Drive Unit)

1. Insert the DOS disk in Drive A.

2. Answer the A> screen prompt by entering
   format a: for double-sided disks only

3. The following message will appear:
   Insert new diskette for drive A:
   and strike any key when ready

   When the in-use lights have stopped blinking, remove your DOS diskette and insert the diskette to be formatted into Drive A.

4. When the process is completed, the screen shows this message:
   Formatting. . .Format complete
      xxxxxx bytes total disk space
      yyyyyy bytes available on disk
   Format another (Y/N)?

5. If you answer Y for yes, the screen instructions repeat; replace the disk with another disk to be formatted.

6. If you answer N for no, the A> prompt reappears.

   NOTE: To save time, format several disks at a
              time.

To Format a Disk (Double-Disk-Drive-Unit)

1. Insert the DOS disk in drive A.

2. Answer the A> screen prompt by entering:
   format b: (double sided)

3. Press RETURN.

4. The screen shows this message:
    Insert new diskette for drive B:
    and strike any key when ready.

5. When the process is completed, the screen shows this message:
    Formatting. . .Format complete
      xxxxxx bytes total disk space
      yyyyyy bytes available on disk
    Format another (Y/N)?

6. If you answer *Y* for yes, the screen instructions repeat; replace the disk in Drive B with another disk to be formatted.

7. If your answer is *N* for no, the A> screen prompt reappears.

Appendix D

Menu Summary — Word Processor

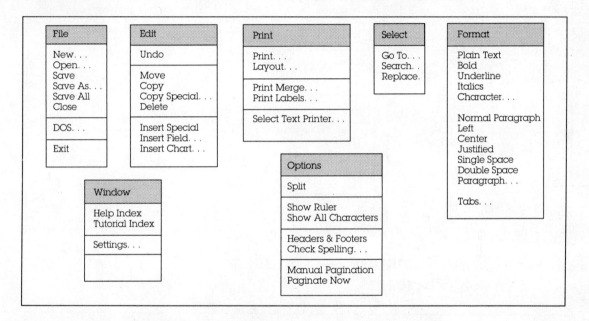

File	Edit	Print	Select	Format
New...	Undo	Print...	Go To...	Plain Text
Open...		Layout...	Search..	Bold
Save	Move		Replace.	Underline
Save As...	Copy	Print Merge...		Italics
Save All	Copy Special...	Print Labels...		Character...
Close	Delete			
		Select Text Printer...		Normal Paragraph
DOS...	Insert Special			Left
	Insert Field...			Center
Exit	Insert Chart...			Justified
				Single Space
				Double Space
				Paragraph...

Window

Help Index
Tutorial Index

Settings...

Options

Split

Show Ruler
Show All Characters

Headers & Footers
Check Spelling...

Manual Pagination
Paginate Now

Format (continued)

Tabs...

NOTE: On all window menus, Help Index and Tutorial
Index appear but are not included on the educational version
of the disk.

■■■■■Menu Summary — Spreadsheet

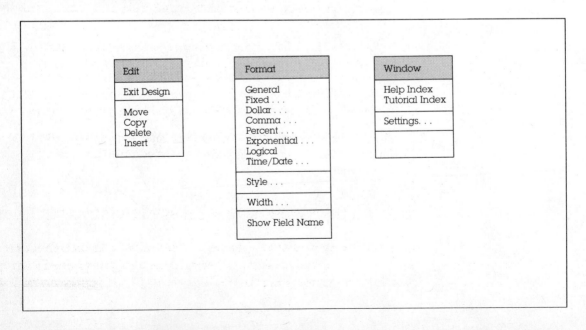

File
New. . .
Open. . .
Save
Save As. . .
Save All
Close

DOS. . .

Exit

Edit
Move
Copy
Copy Special. . .
Clear
Delete
Insert

Fill Right
Fill Down

Name. . .

Print
Print. . .
Layout. . .

Set Print Area
Insert Page Break
Delete Page Break
Font. . .

Print Chart. . .

Select Text Printer. . . .

Select
Row. . .
Column. . .

Go To. . .
Search. . .

Format
General
Fixed . . .
Dollar . . .
Comma . . .
Percent . . .
Exponential . . .
Logical . . .
Time/Date . . .

Style . . .

Width. . .

Options
Freeze Titles
Unfreeze Titles
Split

Show Formulas
Protect

Manual Calculation
Calculate Now

Chart
Define
New
View

Charts. . .

Window
Help Index
Tutorial Index

Settings. . .

■■■■■Menu Summary — Database
Design Screen:

Edit
Exit Design

Move
Copy
Delete
Insert

Format
General
Fixed . . .
Dollar . . .
Comma . . .
Percent . . .
Exponential . . .
Logical
Time/Date . . .

Style . . .

Width . . .

Show Field Name

Window
Help Index
Tutorial Index

Settings. . .

Form Screen:

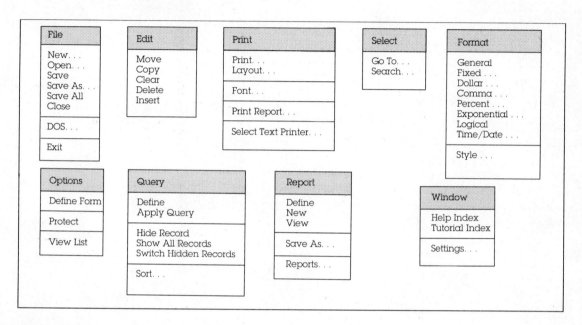

Menu Summary — Communications

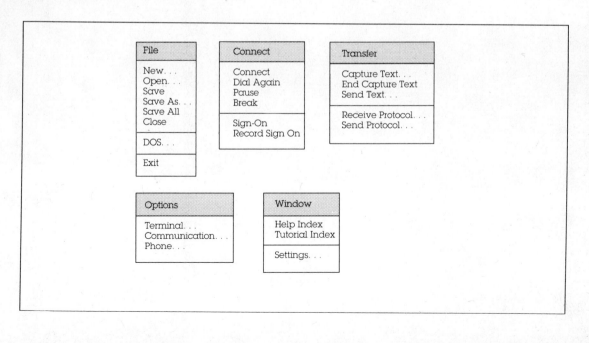

Appendix E

Application Exercises

Word Processing Applications

Directions: Using your word-processing software, complete the following applications. Proofread and correct all typographical errors. Save each file using the name given. Print copies according to your instructor's directions.

Application 1

Type the following letter. Proofread and correct all typographical errors. Name the file RENTAL.

(Use Current Date)

Mr. Grant Wilson
1243 Fairmont Street
Grand Prairie, TX 75052

Dear Mr. Wilson:

Effective at 6 p.m. on November 21, 19--, we will close our facility at 1401 E. Traffic Way. We are merging the downtown shop and rental operations into our facility at 2461 Neergard, which is one block north of Coit Road on Valley View Lane.

Our administrative offices (including sales and safety) will be located at 1320 South Glenstone, Suite 24.

I have enclosed a supply of stickers with our new telephone numbers on them. Please distribute these to persons within your business who will be calling on us.

We would like to thank you for your patience during this transition. We will make every effort to ensure that you receive the same quality service you have enjoyed in the past.

Sincerely,

GIBSON TRUCK RENTAL, INC.

Jerry Dearborne
District Manager

xx

Enclosures

Application 2

Retrieve the file named RENTAL and make the following changes. Save the file under the same name again.

(Use Current Date)

Mr. Grant Wilson
1243 Fairmont Street
Grand Prairie, TX 75052

Dear Mr. Wilson:

Effective at 6 p.m. on ~~November 21,~~ August 15 19--, we will close our facility at 1401 E. Traffic Way. We are merging the downtown shop and rental operations into our facility at 2461 ~~Neergard,~~ Davon which is one block north of Coit Road on Valley View Lane.

Our administrative offices (including sales and safety) will be located at 1320 South Glenstone, Suite ~~24.~~ 36

I have enclosed a supply of stickers with our new telephone numbers on them. Please distribute these to persons ~~within your business~~ who will be calling on us.

We would like to thank you for your patience during this transition. We will make every effort to ensure that you receive the same quality service you have enjoyed in the past.

Sincerely,

GIBSON TRUCK RENTAL, INC.

Jerry Dearborne
District Manager

xx

Enclosures

Application 3

Type the following document. Proofread and correct all typographical errors. Name the document CARS.

(Use Current Date)

Mr. & Mrs. Bailey Stevens
2155 Markham Avenue
Dallas, TX 75222

Dear Mr. & Mrs. Stevens:

Enclosed is a questionnaire relating to the car you drive most often. Please complete the questionnaire and return it as soon as possible in the postage-paid envelope provided. It will take you only a few minutes to do this.

We are gathering information from representative car owners in the Dallas/Fort Worth area--people like yourself. The automotive industry is very interested in your opinions, which can play a vital role in shaping the car designs of the future.

Because we are contacting a limited number of car owners, your cooperation in completing and returning the questionnaire will be very much appreciated. Information you furnish will be treated as <u>strictly confidential</u>.

Sincerely,

James Miller
Chairman of the Board
Automotive Research

xx

Enclosures

Application 4

Retrieve the file named CARS. Change the margins to left 2 inches (position 20) and right 1 1/2 inches (position 70). Save the file under the same name.

Application 5

Type the following document. Name the file PAYMENT.

(Use Current Date)

May we remind you...

A few days ago we notified you that a payment was due. We have yet to hear from you.

We have always appreciated the fine manner in which you have paid on your account. If you are experiencing financial difficulties, please contact us. You are eligible to apply for additional money. We are always very willing to help you. If you are certain that we cannot help you at this time, please mail or bring your payment into our office today.

If we can be of assistance to you in the future, never hesitate to call or stop in to see us.

Sincerely,

Manager

xx

Application 6

Retrieve the file named PAYMENT. Make the following changes. Save the file under the same name again.

(Use Current Date)

∧ Dear Ms. Reynolds:
May we remind you...

Send this letter to:
Ms. Joyce Reynolds
4709 Hickory St.
Texarkana, AR 75502

A few days ago we notified you that a payment was due. We have yet to hear from you.

We have always appreciated the fine manner in which you have paid on your account. If you are experiencing financial difficulties, please contact us. You are eligible to apply for additional money. We are always very willing to help you. If you are certain that we cannot help you at this time, please mail or bring your payment into our office today.

If we can be of assistance to you in the future, never hesitate to call or stop in to see us.

Sincerely,

∧ — Bill Green
Manager

▰▰▰▰ Spreadsheet/Graphics Applications

Directions: Using your spreadsheet software, complete the following applications. Your applications may appear differently on your screen than shown here. Adjust the headings and column widths as necessary. Save each file using the name given. Print copies according to your instructor's directions.

Application 1

Create the following sales summary as a spreadsheet. Enter formulas to total the sales of each department. Name the file SUMMARY.

GASTON DEPARTMENT STORE

Sales Summary, March 31, 19--

	Department A	Department B	Department C
	$ 1,223.14	$ 2,112.99	$ 3,221.66
	544.50	659.88	3,445.00
	981.10	1,256.00	333.90
	2,421.30	4,578.25	921.40
	322.80	452.60	1,900.00
Total			

Application 2

Create the following inventory schedule as a database. Name the file BEDFORD.

J. D. BEDFORD & SON

Furniture & Equipment Inventory

MONTH	DAY	YEAR	DESCRIPTION	COST	INV NO
Feb	3	88	File Cabinet	480.00	33299
Feb	15	88	Desk and Chair	880.00	23338
Mar	20	88	Typewriter	995.00	34566
Apr	1	88	Typewriter	750.00	86444
May	9	88	Calculator	180.00	15543
Jun	3	88	Computer	2650.00	98990
Jul	21	88	Computer Table	275.00	22211
Jul	21	88	Printer	1995.00	55432
Aug	12	88	Printer Table	250.00	98777
Sep	4	88	File Cabinet	440.00	32112

Application 3

Create the following spreadsheet. Enter the formulas to total each row. Name the file HOLLOW.

OAK HOLLOW HOMEOWNERS ASSOCIATION

Association Dues, 1988-89

Homeowner	Johnson	Barrett	Smith	Reynolds	Green	Totals
Amt. Due	$30.00	$22.50	$15.00	$50.00	$17.50	
Amt. Paid		15.00	15.00	25.00	17.50	
Bal. Due	30.00	7.50		25.00		

Application 4

Retrieve the file named SUMMARY; insert a row before the "Total" row and add the information shown below; then recalculate the totals. Name the revised file SUMMARY.

	Department A	Department B	Department C
	4,321.50	10,500.30	6,443.98
Total			

Application 5

Retrieve the file named BEDFORD. Insert a column between "YEAR" and "DESCRIPTION"; then insert the information below in the blank column created. Name the revised copy INV.

SERIAL NO.

222 BJ 2211

900223

2278-1212

990-3222

09983221

JJL223

48-48-09

221JN

4657-1

B-50

Application 6

Create the following spreadsheet. Enter formulas to compute the total price for each item, the grand total, and total number sold by entering the formulas in the appropriate cells. Name the file SALES.

HARTS WINDOW TREATMENTS

Item No.	Sale Price	Number Sold	Total Price
K332-34	350.80	25	
L21-55	155.95	17	
J90-09	225.50	80	
M212-5	88.95	21	
B-56-3	125.25	32	
Total			

Application 7

Create the following spreadsheet. Enter a formula to calculate the total sales. Create a pie chart from the spreadsheet. Save the spreadsheet and pie chart. Name the file SOFTWARE.

DISCOUNT SOFTWARE WORLD

Software Sales, July, 19--

WordPerfect	1231
WordStar	1008
Microsoft Word	1743
MultiMate Advantage	899
DisplayWrite 4	764
TOTAL	

Directions for creating a pie chart: Use the information below to create a pie chart from the spreadsheet you just completed. Check the pie chart by viewing it.

1. Purpose: To show visually how many copies of each software was sold by brand as a percent of the whole.

2. Main title: DISCOUNT SOFTWARE WORLD

3. Sub-title: Software Sales, July, 19--

4. Graph name: Name the graph according to your instructor's directions

Application 8

Create the following spreadsheet. Enter formulas to calculate the total amount of snow and rain for the six months. Create a line graph from the spreadsheet. Save the spreadsheet and line graph. Name the file SNOWFALL.

WEATHER REPORT-CENTRAL PLAINS REGION

January 1 - June 30, 19--

	JAN	FEB	MAR	APR	MAY	JUN	TOTAL
Snow (Feet)	6.5	7.9	3.8	1.1	.8	.05	
Rain (Inches)			1.3	4.7	3.9	5.11	

Directions for creating a line graph: Use the following information from the spreadsheet you just completed to create a line graph. Check the graph by viewing it.

1. Purpose: To show the increase and decrease visually of the snowfall in the Central Plains Region from January 1 to June 30, 19--.

2. Main title: WEATHER REPORT-CENTRAL PLAINS REGION

3. Sub-title: January 1 - June 30, 19--

4. Graph name: Name the graph according to your instructor's directions

Application 9

Retrieve the file named SNOWFALL and create a bar graph to show the rainfall amounts. Check the graph by viewing it.

1. Purpose: To show visually the increases and decreases in rainfall by month for the Central Plains Region during January 1 -June 30, 19--

2. Main title: WEATHER REPORT-CENTRAL PLAINS REGION

3. Sub-title: January 1 - June 30, 19--

4. Graph name: Name the graph according to your instructor's directions

Application 10

Create the following spreadsheet. Enter a formula to calculate the total. Create a pie chart from the spreadsheet. Save the spreadsheet and pie chart. Name the file DPE.

DELTA PI EPSILON

19-- State Conference

City	Attendance
Abiline	8
Brownwood	2
Carthage	3
Dallas	15
Fort Worth	18
Houston	25
Tyler	4
TOTAL	

Directions for creating a pie chart: Use the information below to create the chart. Check the pie chart by viewing it.

1. Purpose: To show visually the attendance at the 19-- State Delta Pi Epsilon Conference by city

2. Main title: DELTA PI EPSILON

3. Sub-title: 19-- State Conference

4. Graph name: Name the graph as your instructor directs.

Database Management Applications

Directions: Using your database software, complete the following applications. Your applications may appear differently on your screen than shown here. Adjust the column headings and widths as necessary. Save each file using the name given. Print copies according to your instructor's directions.

Application 1

Create the following database using columns A to C. Sort the database in ascending order by city office. Name the file PUBLIC.

CITY OFFICE	PHONE NO.	NAME
City Manager	780-5017	Kevin Smith
Assistant City Manager	780-4000	Betty Cimeron
City Secretary	780-5004	Jim Davis
Director of Finance	780-5005	Ruth Willis
Director of Personnel	780-5070	Janet Morgan
Director of Purchasing	780-0001	Brent Woodward
Tax Office	780-3211	Dianna Harwood
Fire chief	780-2333	John Willingham
Police Chief	780-2020	Ralph Harris
Director of Public Works	780-3233	Jess Parkhill

Application 2

Create a database giving the name, office, street address, city, state, zip code, area code, and phone number for the following people with offices in your city or state. Name the file OFFICIAL. After the database is created, search and find the name of your congressman; your fire chief; your police chief.

Each senator	Your fire chief
Each congressman	Your police chief
Your mayor	Your county tax assessor
Your city manager	Your U.S. Postmaster

You may add any offices unique to your city or state or delete any not applicable.

Application 3

Create the following database. Sort the file by last name in ascending order. Name the file FACULTY. Extract and print a copy of the names of the members of the Auditing Committee.

LAST	FIRST	MI	COLLEGE	COMMITTEE	DEPARTMENT
Cox	Steven	F	Brookhaven	Auditing	Accounting
Blair	Emmeline	A	Del Mar	Registration	English
Allen	Enrique	K	Houston	Legislative	Government
Page	Michael	B	Tyler	Membership	PE
Kerr	Roger	L	Austin	Nominating	Marketing
Clere	Thomas	J	Houston	Registration	English
Green	Lawanda	W	Weatherford	Membership	Drama
Hurst	Edith	I	Midland	Resolutions	Accounting
Cox	Leticia	R	El Centro	Auditing	Art
Hall	Alden	P	Hill County	Social	Mathematics
Ford	Alyce	A	Brazosport	Editorial	Reading
Lobb	Gerald	C	Odessa	Editorial	Physics

Peters	Leroy	B	Houston	Social	History
Bailey	Joyce	R	San Antonio	Legislative	English
Burns	Linda	M	St Phillips	Auditing	PE

Application 4

Create the following database. Sort the database in ascending order by last name. Name the file ROSTER.

LAST	FIRST	MI	ADDRESS	CITY	STATE	ZIP
O'Kurma	Charles	D	1232 Crayton St.	Dallas	TX	75080
Dudley	Nancey	M	5342 Morgan St.	Ft. Worth	TX	76119
Raye	Susan	K	8900 Harry Hines	Dallas	TX	75223
O'Neal	Stan	J	2932 Forrest Ln.	Dallas	TX	75232
Hudspeth	Laura	P	1233 Dumont Ln.	Richardson	TX	75080
King	Carol	A	1332 Western St.	Arlington	TX	76101
Duryea	June	N	8080 Martin Dr.	Dallas	TX	75422
Spurlock	Bill	J	1919 Blair Dr.	Ft. Worth	TX	75542
Jacobs	Bryan	L	3233 Cooke Ln.	Richardson	TX	75086
Attner	Lee	V	2211 Forshee St.	Dallas	TX	75544
Patton	Terry	I	126 Dutton Dr.	Arlington	TX	76011

Application 5

Add the following employees to the file named ROSTER; then resort the file in ascending order by last name.

LAST	FIRST	MI	ADDRESS	CITY	STATE	ZIP
Brown	Janet	K	2211 Hilcrest St.	Ft. Worth	TX	76244
Grant	Hazel	T	201 Jackson St.	Ft. Worth	TX	76787
Puerta	Maria	I	477 Campus Dr.	Ft. Worth	TX	76119

| Jones | Peggy | S | 909 Beckley Dr. | Ft. Worth | TX | 76331 |
| Jacobs | Billy | V | 551 Riverside Dr. | Ft. Worth | TX | 76001 |

Application 6

Create the following database. Name the file TITLES.

TITLE	AUTHOR	COPYRIGHT
Affluent Americans	Winters, R. R.	1985
Auditing Made Easy	Jeters, P. L.	1985
Business: Tomorrow's Future	Ramsey, J. T.	1988
Contemporary Business Relations	Zimmerman, L.I.	1988
Essentials of Business	Hartley, F. M.	1989
Fundamentals of Management	Cullen, R. W.	1988
Practical Administration	Venzor, R. Q.	1989

Insert a row after "Contemporary Business Relations" and add the following information under each appropriate heading:

TITLE	AUTHOR	COPYRIGHT
Delusion: The American Economy	Winters, R. R.	1989

Application 7

Retrieve the file named TITLES. Sort the author's names in ascending order. Add a column after "AUTHOR"; title it COPIES SOLD. Leave it blank.

Application 8

Create the following database. Sort the database in ascending order. Name the file WILSON. Extract the names of those people who watched "One is Enough" on July 15.

NAME	TIME	TV SHOW WATCHED	NETWORK
Wilson, George	7:00	One is Enough	CBC
Wilson, George	7:30	Run for Your Money	NBB
Sanders, Maria	6:00	Bad Day in Georgetown	NBB
Sanders, Maria	7:30	Great is My Worth	NBB
McAvoy, Bill	8:00	Best of Everything	CBC
McAvoy, Bill	8:30	You Are For Me	CBC
Martin, J. T.	6:30	Bet Your Savings	NBB
Kennedy, B.T.	7:00	One is Enough	CBC
Kennedy, B.T.	7:30	Run for Your Money	NBB
Rutledge, R. R.	7:00	One is Enough	CBC
Rutledge, R. R.	7:30	Wheel of Tomorrow	AAB
Lewis, Mark	7:00	One is Enough	CBC
Bryan, F. D.	8:00	The Betty Sutton Story	NBB

Application 9

Create the following database. Sort the file by name in ascending order and print one copy. Name the file RETIRE. Sort the file by date retired and print one copy.

NAME	DEPARTMENT	YEAR RETIRED
Sartain, J. J.	Personnel	1980
Cockerham, Dianne	Engineering	1979
Johnston, Jr., N. E.	Marketing	1951
Reed, Joey	Maintenance	1965

Allen, William	Communications	1977
Hairston, Carlos	Safety	1984
Gladden, W. W.	Purchasing	1966
Murphy, Carol A.	Engineering	1988
Shockley, Durward	Marketing	1990

Application 10

Create the following database. Sort the file by last name in ascending order. Name the file MORGAN. Search and find the customers with a $2,000 credit limit.

NAME	ADDRESS	ACCT NO	CR LIMIT
Brock, Bill	221 Crestmont St.	6060-10	$ 1000
Vaughan, Frank	114 Ridgeway St.	6022-34	$ 500
Fulton, Mildred	875 Morgan Dr.	6033-63	$ 1500
Miller, Ruth P.	909 Reading Ln.	6026-89	$ 1000
Parks, Donald	1212 Brandon Dr.	6033-33	$ 300
Thomas, Malcolm	1514 Beardon St.	6077-21	$ 2000
Trout, Ira	322 Pendelton St.	6021-16	$ 500
Laird, Bertha	199 Hargrove Dr.	6038-09	$ 2000
Boothe, Margaret	221 Bennington Ln.	6022-88	$ 1500
Finch, Ethel	9986 Portland St.	6066-29	$ 300

Application 11

Retrieve the file named FACULTY and delete all members of the Editorial Committee. Save the file again under the same name.

Application 12

Retrieve the file named MORGAN. Insert a column after "ACCT NO" and insert the following information:

ACCT BALANCE

$ 449.60

$ 322.00

$ 1090.55

$ 950.25

$ 185.13

$ 1933.56

$ 449.66

$ 87.05

$ 326.80

$ 72.11

Save the file again under the name MORGAN.

■■■■■■ Telecommunications Applications

Directions: Using your Microsoft Works communications tool, complete the following applications. Your applications may appear differently on the screen than shown here. Check with your instructor for additional information as needed to complete these exercises.

Application 1

Create a communication file for a local information service. Name the file the name of the service and save the file.

Application 2

Using the communication file you just created for a local information service in Application 1, log on to the service following your instructor's directions. After logging on, browse around the information available, then disconnect from the service.

Application 3

Create a communication file to connect with another computer. Ask your instructor for the various settings needed such as baud rate, databits, stopbits, handshake, parity, and port. Name and save the file.

Application 4

Using the communication file you created in Application 3, make a connection with the host computer and key and display text by asking and then answering the following questions. Make certain the host computer is set to answer.

1. What is the greatest advantage to having telecommunications equipment and software in an office?

2. In what way might an office utilize an information service?

3. What are the advantages and disadvantages for connecting several computers to one another using telecommunications?

Application 5

Using the communication file you created in Application 3, set your computer to answer. Have the host computer contact you. Ask the host computer three questions of your choice.

Application 6

Type the following paragraph using the word processing part of your software. Name the file CAPTURE and save it. (Then follow the instructions on the next page.)

You can receive information (called downloading) from another computer two ways. The Capture Text command saves the information that appears on your screen in a file so that later you can print, edit, or include it in another file. The Receive Protocol command allows you to receive a file transferred from another computer to a file on your disk.

After the file is named and saved, open the host computer's communication file you created in Application 3 and use the Send Protocol command and send the file named CAPTURE to the host computer's disk. Make certain the host computer is set to answer and that the Receive Protocol command is used. Have the host computer name the file CAP. Ask the host computer to type you a message on the screen once the file is received. The file CAP should appear on the host computer's directory.

Application 7

Disconnect from the host computer's communication session.

Application 8

Reverse the procedure outlined in Application 6 and set your computer to receive the file named CAP using the Receive Protocol command. Name the file to be received CAP2. Check your directory for the file name CAP2 and send a message to the host computer explaining you received the file.

Application 9

Disconnect from the host computer's connection.

Application 10

Close all communication files.

Application 11

Using your word processing tool, type the following memorandum. Name the file WAIVER. Open the communication file created in Application 3 and connect. Send the memorandum to the host computer. Make certain the host computer is set to answer; the host computer is to name the file GARCIA.

INTEROFFICE MEMORANDUM

To: Julian Shepherd, Director of Personnel

From: Lee Judson, Assistant Finance Director

Subject: Request for Waiver to Recruiting Procedures

Date: September 1, 19--

Rio Garcia has worked for us part time for three years. During this time her duties have included typing, filing, acting as a terminal operator on a CRT, processing mail and doing a variety of related special projects. She has demonstrated she is a reliable, conscientious employee.

We have a Clerk II position which just became vacant unexpectedly and Ms. Garcia has expressed an interest in becoming a full-time City employee.

This is a request for your approval to transfer her from her current part time position to a permanent Clerk II position effective the beginning of the first pay period in the new fiscal year.

Application 12

Using your spreadsheet tool, create the following partial spreadsheet using columns A to F. Calculate earnings (cells F5 to F9); calculate total regular hours (B10), overtime hours (C10), total hours (D10), total earnings (F10). Name the file UNIVERSL. Send the file to your host computer. Ask the host computer to name the file UMC.

	A	B	C	D	E	F
1	UNIVERSAL MANUFACTURING COMPANY					
2	Payroll Period Ending, June 30, 19--					
3						
4	EMPLOYEE	REG HRS	OT HRS	TOTAL	HRLY RATE	EARNINGS
5	Crow, J.J.	40	10	50	$6.50	
6	Craig, L.M.	40	5	45	$7.75	
7	Gunn, Betty	40	11	51	$8.40	
8	Dailey, Ralph	40	0	40	$7.95	
9	Jude, Rita	40	8	48	$8.80	
10	Totals					

Application 13

Using your database tool, create the following database using columns A to
F. Sort the file in ascending order. Name the file EMPLOYEE. Connect to your
host computer and send the file. Have the host computer set to answer and
to name the file LIST.

	A	B	C	D	E	F
1	UNIVERSAL MANUFACTURING COMPANY					
2	Employee Roster					
3	EMPLOYEE	ADDRESS	CITY	STATE	ZIP	PHONE
4	Crow, J.J.	212 Hillsdale St.	Dallas	TX	76080	238-8899
5	Craig, L.M.	115 Gene Dr.	Bowie	TX	76010	660-2234
6	Gunn, Betty	2322 Dorsey Dr.	Dallas	TX	75223	772-9988
7	Dailey, Ralph	5522 Holmes St.	Denton	TX	76888	889-3232
8	Jude, Rita	334 Crawford Dr.	Dallas	TX	75808	224-6644

Application 14

Connect to your host computer and ask that the file named UMC be sent back
to you. You are to name it UMC2. Check your directory for the name of the
file, open the file, check it, then close it.

Index